KU-027-261

Spinning

An Leabharlann Chathartha, Corcaigh

Leabharlann Chathair Chorcai

3 0007 00063 600 0

REFERENCE DEPARTMENT

CLASS R 746·1 CRON A/NO 67280

THIS BOOK is provided for use in the Reference Room
only, and must not be taken away. It is earnestly
requested that readers use the books with care, and
do not soil them, or cut, tear or turn down leaves, or
write or make any marks on them or otherwise damage
them. The habit of wetting finger or thumb to turn
leaves should especially be avoided. The use of the
Reference Room is subject to the Rules and Bye-Laws,
and any injury to books, or any improper conduct,
will be dealt with as therein provided.

HB

The Complete Spinning Book

The Complete Spinning Book

by Candace Crockett

WATSON-GUPTILL PUBLICATIONS/NEW YORK

N 67280

Copyright © 1977 by Watson-Guptill Publications

First published 1977 in the United States and Canada by Watson-Guptill
Publications,
a division of Billboard Publications, Inc.
1515 Broadway, New York, N.Y. 10036

Library of Congress Cataloging in Publication Data
Crockett, Candace, 1945-
    The complete spinning book.
    Bibliography: p.
    Includes index.
    1. Hand spinning. I. Title.
TT847.C76   746.1'2   77-2712
ISBN 0-8230-0860-6

All rights reserved. No part of this publication may be
reproduced or used in any form or by any means—graphic,
electronic, or mechanical, including photocopying, recording,
taping, or information storage and retrieval systems—
without written permission of the publishers.

Manufactured in U.S.A.

First Printing, 1977

For my friends and teachers,
Helen Pope, Esther McKinley, and Anne Blinks.

ACKNOWLEDGMENTS

I owe special thanks to Margery Livingston and Ralph Putzker, colleagues of mine at San Francisco State University, and to all my students there—especially to Patricia Christensen, Pheobe McAfee, Ruth Tanenbaum, Joann Joyce, and Linda Watson. The four people most responsible for the inspiration and completion of this book were Helen Pope, Esther McKinley, Anne Blinks, and my sister Leslie Wolcott, who did the illustrations. Spinning wizard Norman Hicks, master wheelwright Alden Amos, and artist-craftsman John Gieling—a dear friend—all contributed more than was asked of them, and are appreciated, I think, more than they know. Especially helpful and responsive to my inquiries were Fumiko Pentler, Margherite Shim-min, Irene Anderson, Jackie Wollenberg, Dina Barzel, Elizabeth Likens, Dorothy Miller, Jerry and Scott Zarbaugh, Lynn and Hal Richardson, Persis Grayson, and Susan Jones, owner of Straw Into Gold. Patricia L. Fiske, assistant curator of the Textile Museum, made the facilities of that fine institution available to me. The writings of E. S. Harrison, the unacknowledged author of a wonderful series of pamphlets published by the National Association of Scottish Woollen Manufacturers, were a constant source of delight and information. I am thankful for his help. Finally, my affection and appreciation to Kent, Christopher, and John, who gave their support and encouragement throughout the project.

Contents

CHAPTER ONE

Notes on the History of Spinning

And sing to those who hold the vital shears,
And turn the adamantine spindle round,
On which the fate of gods and men is wound

From Norse Mythology

An illustration from a medieval manuscript showing typical male and female occupations of the time: the woman spins the thread, and the man tills the soil.

CORK CITY LIBRARY

Spinning was already a very ancient art when Hector, in the *Iliad,* urged Andromache to spin during his absences. Spinning was known—as revealed in the findings of burial sites and tombs and as seen in ancient mosaics, wall paintings, and "clothed" statuary—in civilizations dating from before three thousand B.C., and seems to have developed spontaneously in Europe, Asia, Africa, and the Americas. It is difficult for the modern mind to understand either the ubiquitous presence of the spinner during times past, or of the need for that presence in the daily lives of the majority of citizens. A complete history of spinning would be a history of civilization, and the attempt here is simply to point out some interesting moments in the development of spinning and in spun fibers. A contemporary child hearing the story of Sleeping Beauty, who was put into her deep and long-lasting sleep when pricked by the witch-poisoned tip of her spindle, might quite understandably ask an equally bewildered adult, "What is a spindle?" Such a question, asked by any but a modern child, would have sounded as naive as "What is an automobile?" might sound to us.

Prior to the invention of the spinning jenny by James Hargreaves in 1765, all of the thread that went into all of the fabrics used for any purpose was passed through the fingers of a handspinner, nearly always a woman, on to a hand spindle or self-powered spinning wheel. Even before the invention of the hand spindle, which must rank among the outstanding discoveries of humanity, or the spinning wheel—by any but modern standards an almost magically complex tool—fibers were spun between the fingers or between palm and thigh to provide

Mishnah: And these are the duties the wife performs for her husband. She grinds, bakes, washes, cooks, nurses her child, makes the bed and spins wool. If she has brought one servant with her, she doesn't grind, bake or wash. If she has brought two, she doesn't cook or nurse the child; three, she doesn't make the bed or spin wool; four, she sits in the salon. Rabbi Eliezer says: Even if she has brought a houseful of servants, he should force her to spin wool, because idleness leads to insanity.

the weaver with strong, standard thread. Spindles and spindle whorls that closely resemble the kinds of hand drop spindles still used today—and until recently used very widely throughout the world—have been found in Neolithic ruins and tombs. Although the spinning wheel seems to have appeared at different times and places in the ancient world, it was not widely known or used in Europe until the time of Columbus' voyages of discovery in the late fifteenth century. Unlike the less portable wheel, the hand spindle could be used nearly anywhere or at any time and would allow the spinner to spin while walking, gossiping, or rocking the cradle. One very old story tells of a woman—a good and virtuous woman, of course—who drove the horses before her to be watered at the river while carrying the family water jug on her head, all the while spinning wool on her hand spindle!

Although much faster than the hand spindle, the spinning wheel

did not displace the spindle, nor did it decrease the importance in the lives of many many generations of women of being able to produce fine, strong thread on the spindle. These two handspinning tools have come to us modified, but basically unchanged, from the time when knowledge of their use was a necessity for women in nearly all levels of society. In the Bible, the good woman is one who "layeth her hands to the spindle and her hand holdeth the distaff" (Proverbs 31:19). The Torah names 39 activities forbidden on the day of rest, and thirteen of them are involved with fabricmaking. The Talmud states that spinning and weaving are part of a married woman's duties, and that a female slave who spins is more desirable than one who bakes and cooks. If the fibers were to be produced, then the women had to be kept busy spinning, and such a necessity has influenced attitudes toward work and leisure in many societies. In nearly all early cultures whose fabrics survive, it is

clear that the spinner's work provided her with the material for esthetic expression—the textile arts have always been the primary medium for women's art.

The distaff, which holds the yet-to-be spun fibers in prepared order, was developed very early, along with many other auxiliary tools and paraphernalia associated with spinning. Distaffs and other spinning equipment from all over the world are quite similar—this similarity of tools from widely separated places points up the highly specialized use of spinning equipment.

In those many thousands of years during which civilizations rose and fell, spinning as a skill was passed on from mother to daughter, generation after generation. It is probably safe to assume that during that long time, just about every potentially usable fiber was either used or examined for use by the spinner. The materials most often spun—and spun so successfully that they are still the primary materials of most handspinners—

Although the hand spindle comes in varying sizes and different materials, it nearly always consists of a spindle shaft and weight called a whorl. Small spindles with tiny whorls like the ones shown were used for spinning fine threads. The needles, spindles, and whorls shown above with the plaited weaver's basket are from pre-Columbian Central and South America. (Photograph by David Donoho.)

Neolithic clay whorls decorated in simple designs.

A woman spinning and entertaining a visitor—spinning was done conscientiously in all households. This illustration is copied from a fifteenth-century drawing by Israhel Van Meckernem the Elder.

A woman of ancient Greece spinning with distaff and spindle.

Morning and evening, sleep she drove away,
   Old Platthis—warding hunger from the door,
And still to wheel and distaff hummed her lay
   Hard by the gates of Eld, and bent ana hoar;
Plying her loom until the dawn was gray,
   The long course of Athene did she tread:
With withered hand by withered knee she spun
   Sufficient for the loom of godly thread,
Till all her work and all her days were done.
   And in her eightieth year she saw the wave
Of Acheron—Old Platthis—kind and brave.

The Spinning Woman
by Leonidas of Tarentum

were cotton, wool, flax, and less often silk. The latter are recommended above all others for use by the beginning spinner.

It is difficult to trace the development or movement of the various fibers from one civilization to another, but it is generally believed that the cultivation of flax, from which linen fibers are derived, was first practiced in predynastic Egypt. In Egyptian mythology, it was told that the gods created flax as their first act, before they themselves appeared on earth. The purity of the fibers from the interior of the protected flax stalk and the ease with which they could be bleached contributed to the importance of linen in Egyptian religion. The quality of the linen material used in the body wrappings of the Egyptian dead reflected the social status of the deceased in the afterworld just as it had in life. Wrappings discovered in Egypt are often incredibly fine, some of them containing as many as 540 warp threads to the inch, and measuring as long as 300 yards.

Cotton, like flax, seems to have been cultivated first in the great river valleys of the Nile and the Indus. Also, as with flax, its use as a spinning material predates written history—and probably since that time, cotton has been consistently one of the most important nonfood crops grown by mankind. In each of these major cultures and in the many that followed them, the level of handspinning skills must have been great enough to fill the spinners with pride, and the observer with wonder and respect. The ceremonial threads and fabrics from these ancient civilizations surpass in fineness anything now produced by spinning machinery of the most sophisticated design.

Much later, the famous gossamer muslins of Dacca were so light and fine that they were said to drape "like air" over the human form. Supposedly, this fabric passed easily when drawn through a finger ring and was so fine that it took 73 yards to make up one pound. These threads and fibers were produced by spinners who were working in materials, traditions, and techniques so ancient even to them that, especially in Egypt, a period of two or three hundred years was nothing compared to looking back toward the dim origins of the spinning art.

While the best or most competent of these many generations of spinners produced the threads destined for the garments of their

It is said that a battle between Romans and Persians in the Mesopotamian desert in 53 B.C. was decided when the Persians began to wave very large banners of brightly colored silk, which produced such a "wild and unfamiliar gleam" that the Romans fled the field.

religious leaders and social betters, the business of daily life went on, and the typical citizen went about his or her daily tasks clothed in something not greatly different from the "homespun" of early America many centuries later. It was not until the eighteenth century that a machine—the cotton gin patented in America by Eli Whitney—was invented that could remove the seeds from cotton fibers. Thus we know of at least five thousand years during which every seed removed from cotton was touched by hand, years during which every twist of a spindle or turn of a spinning wheel was spinner-powered, and every garment worn was produced from first to

A contemporary Rumanian woman spinning with spindle and distaff.

Sheep raising was practiced throughout the ancient world. In Greece and Rome, sheep were given individual names, covered with skins in cold weather, and taken to special pastures in the summer. Flocks of sheep represented wealth and power, and, from the beginning, efforts were directed toward improving the quality and quantity of wool produced. Sheep's wool is the fiber most favored by today's spinner.

16

last by the personal energy and diligence that in many cultures came to be represented by the spinner at her work.

Just as cotton and linen were the chosen plant fibers through the centuries, sheep's wool was the most widely used animal fiber in Europe and Asia. Domestication of sheep came early in man's history and was practiced throughout the ancient world. Although other animal fibers, such as those from the yak or llama, were used in the absence of domesticated sheep, wool spun throughout history has for the most part been sheep's wool. It is interesting to note that most modern zookeepers know of some handspinner who has an interest in the wool of the bison, goat, llama, musk ox, or camel. The hair of long-coated dogs is often spun, as is human hair. The peculiar qualities of sheep's wool, though, make it especially satisfactory as a spinning material, and its supremacy as the all-round "best" fiber is generally agreed on.

Sheep have always represented wealth, and efforts were continually made to improve the quality of wool produced. In Roman times, the wool toga was valued for its high quality and fineness. By the time Spain and England became world powers, one of the many areas of competition between the two nations was the very lucrative wool trade. Sometime around the twelfth century, the Spaniards developed the Merino sheep, perhaps through North African strains. These sheep produced fine wool and gave the Spanish a distinct lead in the wool competition for some time. In England, the wool trade became so important in time, that many of that country's customs and laws grew out of the wool commerce. As these developments shaped the customs and traditions of government, trade, agriculture, and social habits in western Europe, sheep and their wool became increasingly important to individuals and cultures throughout the world. The trend in recent years has been toward the establishment of wool as a luxury fiber, a trend brought on by the introduction, cheap mass production, and widespread acceptance of manmade fibers.

It is difficult to clearly illustrate the historical importance of the various fibers, fabrics, dyestuffs, and other textile products—they were not only important in the day-to-day lives of the citizens of nearly all past times, but they were also very important trade goods. As such, they precipitated the establishment of many of the trade routes by way of which all sorts of information and experience was transmitted from civilization to civilization. For example, silk was produced for centuries under the greatest secrecy; it was valuable enough to be used as currency and was available in the West only from traders who as early as 126 B.C. risked bringing the valuable material to Persia, Syria, and Arabia over the so-called silk road, which at 6,000 miles was the longest trade road of the ancient world. Western traders would meet the caravans and barter for the silk in such meeting places as Damascus and Baghdad. It was not until the sixth century A.D. that two Persian missionary monks who had spent many years in China were encouraged by the Byzantine emperor Justinian to smuggle out of China the silkworm eggs and mulberry seeds that were to be the source of the first western silk industry. These eggs and seeds, hidden inside the walking sticks of the two monks, flourished, and the silken textiles of Byzantium became famous and highly valued. By about 1000 A.D. silk production

This drawing is taken from a painting, Female Tasks, by the sixteenth-century-artist Johannes Stradanus. The original painting is on the ceiling of the Palazzo Vecchio in Florence. The theme of transformation, of change, appears frequently, and the spindle or spinning wheel does not just spin fiber into yarn—it spins life into death, straw into gold, and drab into gay.

flourished in India, where, according to legend, the industry grew from seeds and eggs smuggled out of China in the lining of the headdress of a Chinese princess.

Many myths and legends tell how silkworm eggs and mulberry seeds were secretly taken from China to other countries that wanted a silk industry, and none of the myths is likely to be any less believable than some of the stories

of the actual events. Silk, although essentially "finished" as it is spun by the silkworm, is sometimes so fine that one strand alone is almost invisible to the naked eye. In order to make these fine threads usable, the filaments from a number of cocoons must be twisted together. Legend has it that this treatment of the bombyx mori, or silkworm, cocoon was first developed by Si Ling, wife of the emperor Hoang-ti, in 2640 B.C.

The handspinner of today will probably find silk prohibitively expensive, but he or she is most likely to deal with silk in the form known as "waste," shorter lengths of silk broken down from the nearly continuous strands the worm uses to form its cocoon. Silk is now, as it has always been, a luxury fiber, and, although raised wherever there are mulberry trees, it still retains something of the mystery and sophistication of the Orient. It is no coincidence, either, that the highest ranking woman in the land was willing to accept credit for the utilization of the excretion of a worm, for the lightness, luster, and draping qualities of silk were unmatched by any fabric then known. Even two and one half millennia later, in the beginning of the Christian era, raw silk from the Orient was literally worth its weight in gold.

Today's spinner should most definitely be aware of the ancientness and richness of the development of the spinner's art. Any person today who begins to handspin should have some feeling for those many millions of spinners, mostly women, who, from the "beginning of time," have picked, plucked, sheared, or in some way reaped the harvest, prepared it for spinning, spun it, and woven it into some useful and beautiful fabric. Today's spinner can practice the art in a totally different context, with different motivations and different goals, but that link with the past, the knowledge of one's place in the continuing history and

> We are spinning our own fates, good or evil, and never to be undone. Every smallest stroke of virtue or of vice leaves its never so little scar... Nothing we ever do is, in strict scientific literalness, wiped out.
>
> William James

practice of this ancient skill, should serve to enrich the experience and give it special meaning even beyond the joy to be gained from seeing the almost magical emergence of thread from fiber.

Experienced spinners know not only the pleasure of creation, but they are also aware of the feel of the fine or well-used wood that is so often used in spinning equipment, of the good wholesome feeling of the natural oils contained in the material to be spun, and of the joy to be gained from both the sight and the feel of the finished product. Visitors to spinners' homes or studios or to places where handspun thread is available for purchase can seldom resist the temptation to pick up and feel the handspun natural materials. I will suggest many techniques in this text and will occasionally ask you to pay particular attention to some aspect of the act of spinning, but no other points have the overall importance of these: our place in practicing and encouraging the revival of an ancient art, and the esthetic-sensual link between ourselves and the materials and products of spinning.

CHAPTER TWO

Spinning on the Hand Spindle

The laden distaff in the left hand placed,
    With springy coils of snow-white wool was graced:
From which, the right hand length'ning drew,
    That into yarn 'neath nimble fingers grew.
At intervals a tender touch was given,
    By which the spinning disc was onward driven:
Then, when the sinking spindle reached the ground,
    The new-spun yarn around the stem was wound,
Until the hook within the nipping cleft
    Held fast the newly finished length of weft.

From a poem by Catullus

An old man from Palestine spinning on a suspended, or drop, spindle. The spindle has wooden crosspieces rather than the more common round whorl. Once spun, the yarn is wound over and under the crosspieces to form a ball.

A drawing of a beautifully carved Cowichan spindle whorl, 7½" in diameter. It was probably used for spinning heavy wool yarns. The animal carved on the whorl turns and twists back on itself, as does the yarn. Modern Cowichans are noted for their nearly waterproof sweaters knitted from heavy handspun yarn. (National Museum of Natural History, Smithsonian Institution, Washington, D.C.)

Fibers were first drawn out of a mass and twisted by hand without the help of any tool. Although such a process is slow and tedious, it will produce a continuous thread and may legitimately be called a form of spinning. This primitive method is not only slow, but it is also haphazard—and there is a tendency for the yarn to untwist, which makes the whole process awkward even after practice. This inefficient but simple system of producing thread undoubtedly helped clothe many generations of our early ancestors; but near the beginning of the development of man's technology, some person began twisting the thread around a stick. This stick would eventually become the shaft of the later, almost universally used hand spindle. The addition of a weight, perhaps a stone or a bit of mud on the stick, allowed the spinner to work faster and with greater ease. The weight held the stick in place and gave momentum, so the twisting action continued when the hand was removed. This continued spinning freed a second hand to control the amount of fibers drawn out. This simple tool, the hand spindle, consists simply of a shaft and a weight, called a whorl. It has been in use for many thousands of years and has been known from the earliest times. The even simpler methods still survive, but they are more difficult to control and are much slower.

THE DROP SPINDLE

The spindle is used in several ways, sometimes suspended (in which case it is called a drop spindle) and sometimes rested on the floor or in a container. The generally most efficient and popular way of using the spindle is to suspend it.

When the spindle is used as a drop spindle, a thread is attached to it above the whorl (which rests at the lower end of the shaft), wound around the shaft under the whorl, and then looped over the tip. Sometimes the spindle has a hook on the bottom and is used with the whorl on top. The suspended, or drop, spindle is both the twisting and the storage device. As the hand turns the spindle, the thread attached to it twists. Fibers are drawn out from the mass, and, as the twist or spin runs up, the new fibers are caught and secured. When the thread is too long to handle, it is released and wound around the shaft above the whorl.

The manner of spinning, the size of the spindle, and the materials a spindle is made from vary from area to area, but the basic design and function are the same.

HOW TO SPIN ON THE DROP SPINDLE

Spindles and fibers of various kinds are available from all spinning suppliers. Spindles are also easily made and can be constructed from readily available items—for example, a dowel stuck into half a potato or apple can function as a spindle. Knitting needles, pencils, tinker toys, wooden spoons, door knobs, yo-yos, and so on can easily be converted into shafts and whorls. The size and weight of the spindle determine the fineness of the yarn spun, but, whatever its size, the shaft is usually tapered and the whorl should be reasonably well-balanced and rubbed or sanded smooth.

Turned wood pieces designed for use as knobs are especially well-adapted for use as whorls. They have been turned on a wood lathe, which leaves a mark in the exact center, which gives the spindle maker a mark for drilling the hole into which the shaft will be inserted. Such knobs are usually flat on

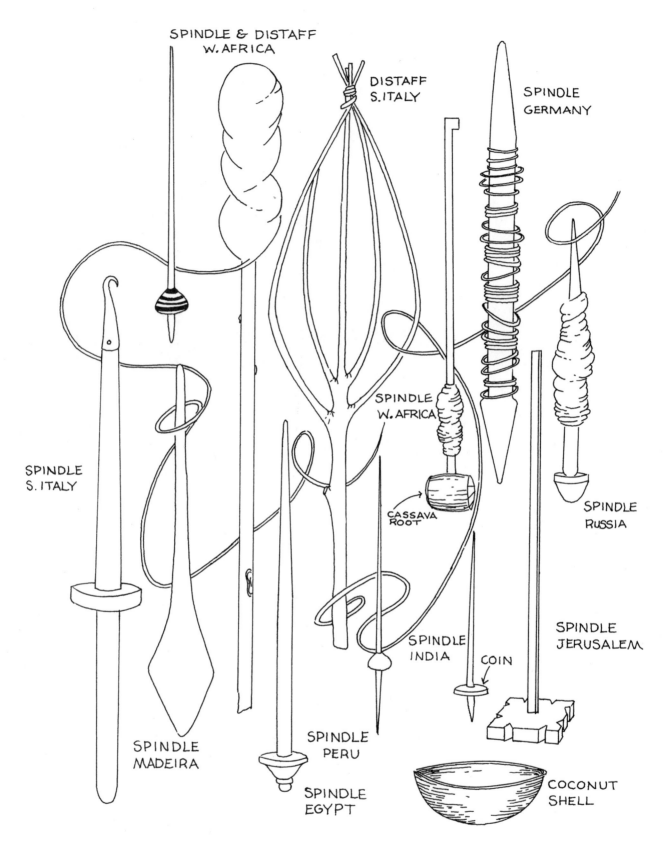

SPINDLE & DISTAFF
W. AFRICA

DISTAFF
S. ITALY

SPINDLE
GERMANY

SPINDLE
W. AFRICA

SPINDLE
S. ITALY

CASSAVA
ROOT

SPINDLE
RUSSIA

SPINDLE
INDIA

COIN

SPINDLE
JERUSALEM

SPINDLE
MADEIRA

SPINDLE
PERU

SPINDLE
EGYPT

COCONUT
SHELL

Spindles and distaffs from different parts of the world. In some instances, the spindle and whorl are carved from solid wood. Some shafts have notches or hooks, while others are tapered to a point or merely left blunt. During spinning, the bottom point of the Indian spindle rests in the coconut shell, since the thread is too fine to support the weight of the spindle. (John Horner Collection, Ulster Museum, Belfast, Ireland.)

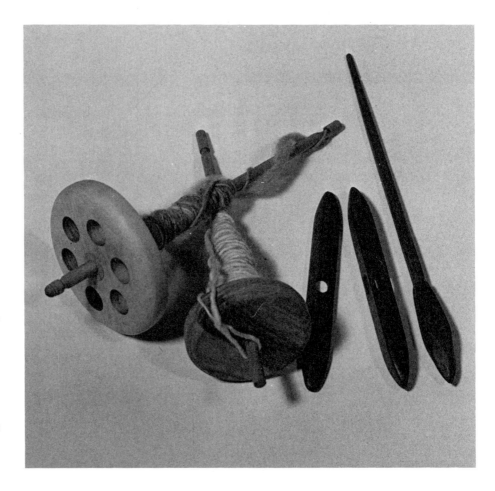

Most contemporary spinners use sturdy wood spindles for spinning medium-fine wool yarns. The whorl on the left spindle is drilled in a balanced pattern that helps efficiency by increasing the percentage of weight near its outer rim. It has a deep vertical groove near the top end of the shaft, which holds and catches the yarn so it does not have to loop around the shaft and under the whorl. The spindle on the right is made up of a center shaft and two crosspieces. One crosspiece fits through the other, and they slip on to the shaft to form a spindle.

The spun yarn is wound to form a ball, and then the crosspieces and ball are lifted off the spindle. When the crosspieces are pulled apart, the ball of yarn is left intact.

one side, and these flat sides make a nice top edge to wind the spun yarn against. The shaft used should be appropriate to the size of the whorl. Shaft ends can be tapered with a knife, file, or pencil sharpener, and some form of notch or groove near the top of the shaft helps hold the thread to the spindle.

Sheep's wool is the most manageable fiber and is strongly recommended for the beginner. It can be greasy or washed, but the individual fibers should have a length of from 3 to 5". Fiber characteristics and special methods of preparation are discussed in later chapters. The spinner has many options as to kind of fiber and state of preparation, but the basic principles of spinning are always the same.

Step 1. To begin, take a hairy, single wool yarn (not a plied yarn) 30" long to use as a starting cord.

Tie the starting cord tightly around the spindle shaft just above the whorl. Turn the spindle a few turns clockwise to anchor the cord.

Step 2. Take the starting cord over the whorl edge and around the shaft where it protrudes under the whorl.

Step 3. Loop the cord over the upper spindle tip by bringing it around the index finger and then shifting it on to the tip. If you hold the cord end, the spindle should dangle, suspended.

Step 4. Take a small cluster of unspun fibers. If the fibers are clumped together pull them apart by teasing. They should be loose, with an equal distribution of air. To begin spinning, hold the end of the starting cord in the left hand between the thumb and forefinger, with the spindle dangling. Overlap a few of the unspun fibers with the starting cord, and give the spindle a clockwise twist at the upper tip with the right hand. (Left-handed spinners may choose to reverse the hands.)

Step 5. Once the fibers become enmeshed (if all else fails, tie a knot) you are off to forming a continuous yarn. Grasp the fibers firmly but gently under your left hand with the right hand and pull down—stretching and drafting the unspun fibers. The space between your two hands, where the unspun fibers are drawn, is the drafting area. The length of this space depends on the length of the fibers. Very short fibers will have a short drafting area, long fibers a correspondingly long drafting area. The drafting area allows the fibers to slide past each other as the right hand draws them down. Your right hand must grasp the fibers firmly to prevent the twist from running up too soon, because when the fibers are twisted they will not draft. If the twist runs up too far, your right hand can untwist to allow the fibers to draw. This untwisting motion prevents clumps, but it is not always necessary. The weight of the spindle stretches the fibers and maintains the tension so the twist runs evenly up the forming thread. Your left hand controls and holds the fiber supply. As your right hand is drawing down, the thumb and fingers of the left hand rub back and forth to spread the fibers, so a triangle of fibers is formed in the drafting zone, with the broad base between the thumb and forefinger of the left hand. This triangular spread prevents the twist from moving too high as the right hand releases the drafted fibers, allowing the twist to move up, spinning the fibers into yarn. The right hand drafts—a large number of fibers for a heavy yarn, and a few for a fine yarn—and then turns the spindle.

Step 6. Continue spinning.

Step 7. Allow the length to extend as far as possible, then slip the end of the spun yarn between the first two fingers of the left hand, and wind the spun yarn in a figure eight motion between your thumb and little finger. This way you will not lose tension on the yarn while winding it on to the spindle shaft. Slip the loop off the spindle tip and off the shaft under the whorl, and then wind the yarn under tension on to the shaft above the whorl by turning the spindle clockwise. Leave enough spun thread to again catch the bottom, and loop over the tip to continue the cycle. As you run out of fibers, add new ones by overlapping loose, unspun fibers. As the yarn accumulates, build it up on the spindle evenly in a cone shape, with the flat whorl-top forming the base. As the spindle fills and becomes too bulky or too heavy for easy spinning, wind the yarn off into balls or skeins. It is possible to dispense with the starting cord and to begin spinning by hooking the unspun fibers over the notched end, turning the spindle to form a beginning.

Basic Principles and Problems. You will become aware of many things as you go through the spinning motions: a thin yarn takes and absorbs twist and is easier to spin than a thick yarn, which seems to reject twist. In unevenly spun yarns, thin places will tend to become tightly twisted, while thick areas will take no twist, remaining lumpy and unspun. This unevenness might well be part of the yarn design, and can be very exciting in yarn when produced by an experienced spinner. If you are a beginner, you should attempt to spin even and uniform medium-fine threads as you practice to develop control.

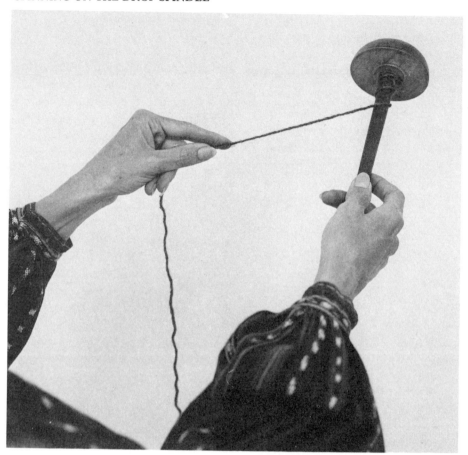

Step 1. Attach the starting cord to the spindle shaft.

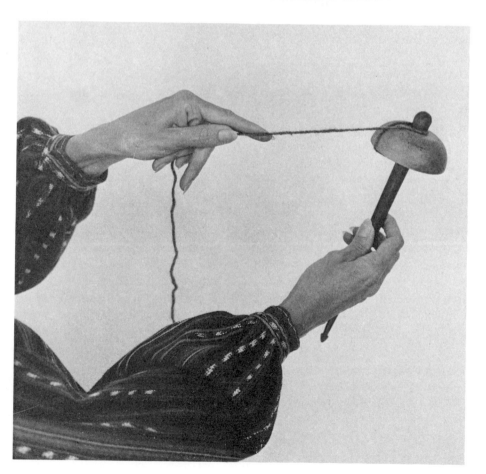

Step 2. Bring the cord over the edge of the whorl and around the shaft.

Step 3. Loop the cord around the finger, and slip the loop over the upper tip of the shaft.

Step 4. Begin spinning by overlapping the unspun, loose fibers with the starting cord. Then turn the spindle to twist them together.

Step 5. Draw the fibers down and then release, allowing the twist from the spinning spindle to move upward.

Step 6. (Above) Continue drafting and twisting until the spindle reaches the floor.

Step 7. Release the yarn and wind it on to the spindle shaft. Leave enough free to again loop around the bottom and over the tip so spinning can continue. Attach new fibers by overlapping.

If your spindle is continually crashing to the floor, it may be too heavy for the yarn you are trying to spin, or it may be spinning backwards at such a rapid rate that the yarn is disintegrating right before your eyes. If you find you are constantly turning the spindle to keep it from unwinding, you are probably trying to spin a too heavy, tightly twisted yarn. Heavy yarns do not need and will not take very much twist—they require a heavy spindle to get up the necessary momentum. If you have this problem, try drawing out fewer fibers. Spinning should be easy, effortless, and rhythmical.

If, after an hour or so, you are straining and tight and uncomfortable, then you must be doing something wrong—so stop, relax, and try again, going very slowly. Hands and spindle are coordinated for smooth spinning, and sometimes it's hard to get the motions in rhythm. Try separating the steps. If the spindle keeps crashing to the floor, try resting its bottom point on a table. If everything is going too fast, hold the spindle between body and table—draw out the fibers, and then, resting the spindle on the table, turn it to spin up the drafted fibers. Stop and draft, then spin again. If there is protruding fuzz, stop, brace the spindle, hold the yarn taut, and pull off the excess. Large lumps in the spun yarn can be grasped at each end, untwisted, and drawn out. When your fingers release the yarn, the twist from the thin areas will move over the newly drafted fibers.

If the yarn is overtwisted, allow the spindle to spin backwards. If you want more twist, twirl the spindle again before continuing. If the yarn is too hairy, move the fingers of your right hand up the yarn as it is twisting, to smooth projecting fibers. A little moisture or oil will sometimes help smooth yarns. Always wind the spun yarn on to the spindle under tension—otherwise it will double back on itself and snag.

With each descent of the spindle, whether turning fast or slowly, the twist distributes equally if the yarn is of uniform thickness. The number of twists per inch in the yarn equals the number of forward revolutions made by the spindle. The long-term regularity of twist and yarn thickness depends on the skill of the spinner and comes with practice.

SPINNING ON THE HEAVY SUPPORTED SPINDLE

Another method, which is generally less efficient than the suspended drop spindle, but which is especially good for sitting and spinning heavy yarns, is used by the Navajo Indians. This method utilizes a very heavy spindle with a long shaft and large whorl. The spinner sits on the ground or on a stool as shown in Step 1. The spindle illustrated has a shaft 36" long and a whorl 6" in diameter. To spin using this method, rest the bottom, or whorl, end of the shaft on the floor or on the ground—if the end slides, place it on a carpet or brace it in some way. Rest the shaft top against your right thigh.

Step 1. Use a starting cord, but do not take it under the whorl as in drop-spindle spinning—instead, wrap it clockwise around the shaft above the whorl. Hold the end of the starting cord in your left hand between thumb and forefinger, and overlap the end with loose unspun fibers. Use your right palm to roll the spindle against the thigh from knee to hip. This rolling action will cause the spindle to rotate in a clockwise direction, causing the fibers to twist. The spindle can also be turned by simply rotating it in

Step 1. Rest the lower end of the spindle on the floor. Turn the spindle against the thigh with one hand, and draw the fibers out with the other as the twist runs up.

a clockwise direction with the fingers of your right hand. As the spindle turns, the left hand draws upward and allows the as yet unspun fibers to slip between thumb and fingers just above and ahead of the twist.

Drafting, or pulling out the fibers, is done with the left hand only, as the right hand turns the spindle. The tension between the left hand and the spindle causes the heavier portions of the twisting yarn to pull and draft out more evenly. It's important to avoid thin sections, because they will take all the twist and leave thicker sections unspun. You can stop turning the spindle at any point to pull or jerk the yarn to stretch out clumps. If the thick sections will not pull out, stop and use both hands to untwist and pull the fibers.

Step 2. When the left arm is fully extended and the fibers twisted, stop, push the spun yarn down on to the spindle, and wind the yarn neatly on to the shaft, leaving just enough to wind around and come off the tip. Navajo spinners traditionally tease and card wool fibers first. The carded fleece is spun once with a minimal amount of drafting and only a light twist. This roving is then spun a second time, and the fibers are fully drafted and twisted to form a firm medium-weight yarn. Many spinners use this kind of spindle for giving machine spun yarn an overtwist, or for spinning two yarns together (called doubling or plying).

OTHER METHODS OF SPINDLE SPINNING

There are other methods of using the spindle that should be mentioned. The suspended spindle is frequently used with the whorl uppermost. Spindles used this way usually have a hook on the bottom that is used to catch the yarn. The shaft is rolled off the spinner's thigh, which sets up a considerable spin. Any spindle can be used this way, but when so used the shaft is longer. How a spindle spins will change when the weight is distributed differently. Changing the position of the whorl or the length of the shaft will adapt a spindle for whorl-uppermost spinning.

If the fibers being spun are very short, as with cotton, or if the yarn is too fine to hold the weight of the spindle, the spinner may choose to support the spindle by resting the tip in a bowl or saucer of some kind.

Spindle whorls are not necessarily round. One widely used spindle style is shown in the illustration on page 24. Rather than a round whorl there are prongs or cross pieces. This is frequently called a Turkish spindle, because it is often used in that country. As the yarn is spun it is wound over and under the prongs to form a ball. On some of these spindles the prongs slip off the shaft and pull apart, leaving the round ball of yarn intact.

In northern Europe a pronged spindle is made in one piece by using the tip of a tree (usually the Christmas tree). The branches form the prongs and clay dabs are put at the ends to give weight.

SPINNING IN GENERAL

The basic motions of spinning are to draw out the fibers to the required fineness, to twist the drafted area to make the thread, and to wind the yarn on to the spindle. The kind and quality of fiber and how it is prepared will determine what the yarn is like. During the spinning process, the spinner has control over the fineness, the smoothness (to a certain extent), and the amount of twist. The fibers are drafted between the hands. The weight of the spindle aids in

Step 2. After drafting and twisting, lower the hand, shift the spindle away from the body, and turn to wind the yarn.

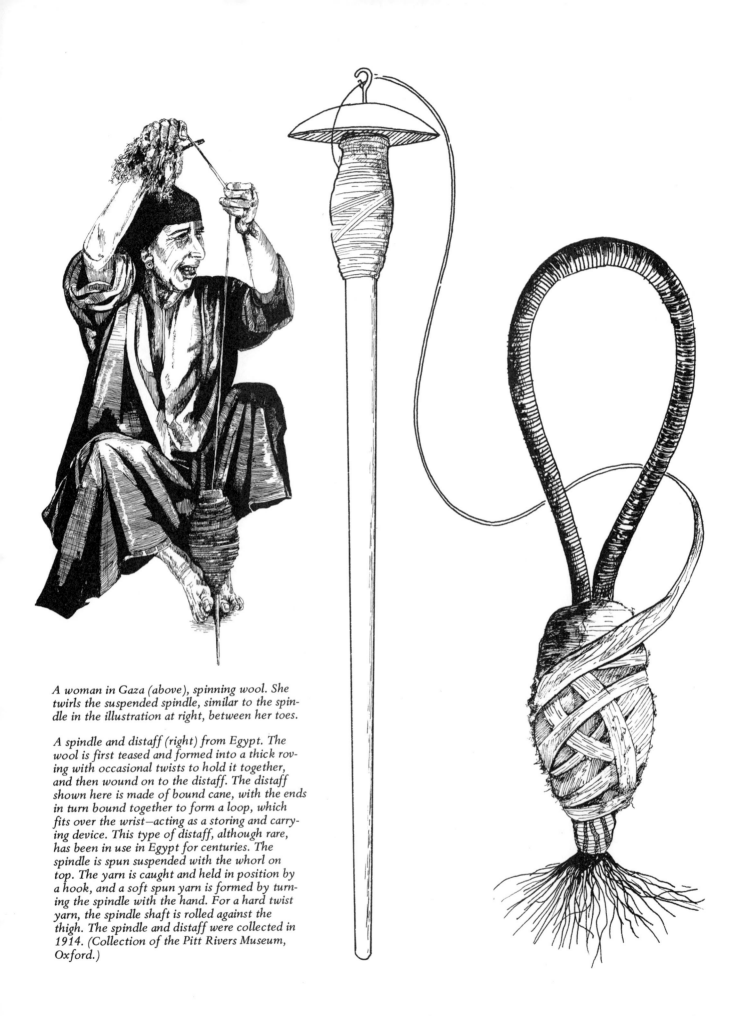

A woman in Gaza (above), spinning wool. She twirls the suspended spindle, similar to the spindle in the illustration at right, between her toes.

A spindle and distaff (right) from Egypt. The wool is first teased and formed into a thick roving with occasional twists to hold it together, and then wound on to the distaff. The distaff shown here is made of bound cane, with the ends in turn bound together to form a loop, which fits over the wrist—acting as a storing and carrying device. This type of distaff, although rare, has been in use in Egypt for centuries. The spindle is spun suspended with the whorl on top. The yarn is caught and held in position by a hook, and a soft spun yarn is formed by turning the spindle with the hand. For a hard twist yarn, the spindle shaft is rolled against the thigh. The spindle and distaff were collected in 1914. (Collection of the Pitt Rivers Museum, Oxford.)

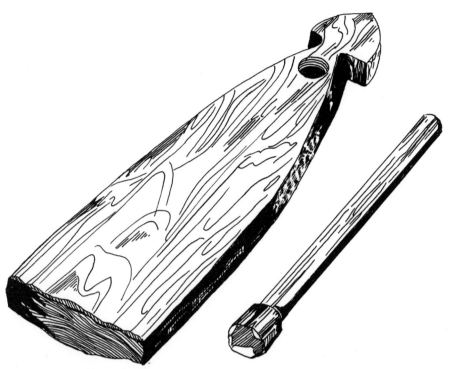

This is a specialized spinning or twisting device used by the Coushatta Indians in Louisiana. It is made of hickory and comes in several sizes; in this example, the longer piece is 13" long. It is used for spinning Spanish moss into a heavy ropelike yarn about an inch thick. The shaft is inserted through the hole and becomes a handle, which is held and rolled in the palm of the hand so the heavy piece, which fits loosely, turns like one arm of a windmill. Fibers are caught on the notched end of the heavy piece by a second person. As the heavy piece spins round and round, the twist runs out along the fibrous moss that is being added as the rope lengthens. The two people gradually get farther and farther apart until the length becomes cumbersome; then that length of spun moss rope is removed, and a new one is begun.

This spinning device from the Canary Islands is a crude spindle mounted horizontally. The spindle is turned by rubbing the hand over the wood handle. The whorl is an iron wheel, and the metal supports are iron. It might have been used to make coarse ropes, with one person turning the spindle and a second person controlling the fibers. A hand drill, electric drill, or egg beater could be used to impart twist in much the same way. (John Horner Collection, Ulster Museum, Belfast, Ireland.)

(Above) A drawing from a medieval illustration showing a woman spinning with distaff and spindle. The European distaff is usually held under the left arm. Although a distaff can hold any kind of fiber supply, it is traditionally used in Europe to hold long flax fibers. "Dis" means bunch of flax in Old English. The "distaff," or spindle, side of a family always refers to the female side, as opposed to the "spear," or male, side. The word distaff is often further generalized, referring to women's work and concerns in general.

(Right) A contemporary hand-carved Greek distaff and spindle.

this drafting by stretching the fibers, and the fingers of both hands work accordingly. As you practice spindle spinning and gain both competence and confidence, you will begin to develop a comfortable and efficient personal spinning style. Vary your stance, reach, spindle speed, thread thickness, and size of spindle. Among experienced spinners, spinning styles vary from the conservative to the very flamboyant. Some spinners even develop the ability to twirl yarn and spindle over their heads much as a cowboy spins his lasso. Don't be afraid to experiment.

THE DISTAFF

A distaff is any tool that holds the supply of raw fibers for the spinner during spinning. It is a convenient tool but usually not necessary. It is most often used for flax, because flax fibers can be long and difficult to manage. In Europe, where it is most widely used, the distaff is usually 10 to 40" long and is held under the left arm or with the end stuck into the spin-

ner's belt. The unspun, prepared fibers are loosely tied to the distaff, wound around it, or simply crammed on to it so they may be drawn out as needed. The distaff has been used since classical times and comes in a marvelous variety of shapes and sizes. As life became more sedentary, the distaff took on new forms; some were designed to be anchored on to benches and some to fit into spinning wheels. The distaff is also found in the form of a tall pole on a stand—this entire mechanism is called a rock, and, like most European distaffs, is used for holding flax fibers.

SKEINING

If the spun yarn is to be washed, dyed, or the twist set, it should be formed into a skein, which is a loose circular arrangement of yarn. The simplest way of making a skein is to wind the spun yarn off in a circular motion between hand and elbow. Any two anchor points, such as C-clamps, chair back, or hands, will also work.

A simple tool called the niddy-

Various niddy-noddy's used for making skeins of yarn. One set of arms on each niddy-noddy are at right angles to the other set, so the spun yarn can be wound to form a measured skein. Most niddy-noddy's have a release device that allows the completed skein to be slipped off easily.

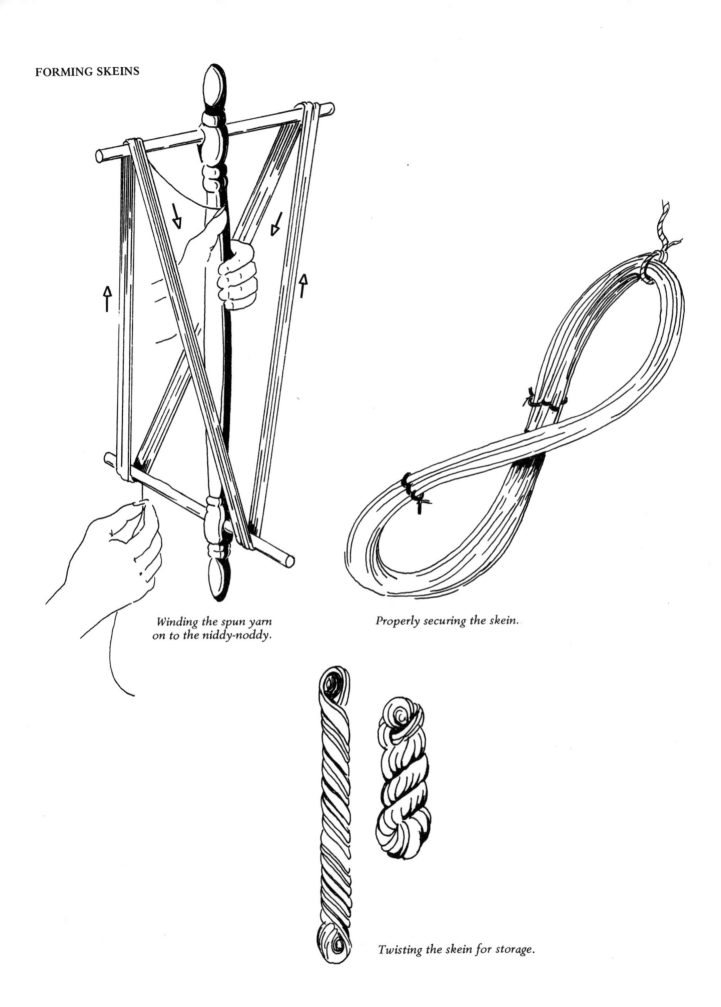

*Winding the spun yarn
on to the niddy-noddy.*

Properly securing the skein.

Twisting the skein for storage.

noddy is sometimes used for forming skeins—uniform skeins of a specific length may be made by using this instrument. Various niddy-noddies are shown in the illustration on page 35, and how they are used is shown in the illustration on page 36. To use the tool, release the yarn from the spindle and hold the yarn end with the left hand, close to the upright section of the tool. Let the spindle roll around on the floor or lie in a basket as you shift the niddy-noddy with your left hand. Your right hand should guide the yarn over its circular path. A special rhyme is often repeated as the yarn is being wound, to help keep track of the yardage:

Niddy noddy, niddy noddy,
Two heads, one body,
Here's one, 'Tain't one,
'Twill be one, bye and bye
Here's two, 'tain't two,
'Twill be two, bye and bye. (etc.)

One round of the niddy-noddy is often one measured yard, so the singer of the rhyme knows how many rounds the yarn has made and how many yards have been wound. Other methods of reeling and winding yarn are discussed in Chapter 4.

Whatever the method used to produce the circular arrangement, the skein must be carefully tied off to prevent unwinding or tangling. To secure the skein properly, the yarn ends should be tied together and attached to a separate length of yarn, which is bound loosely around the skein at that point, and then tied on itself. This technique allows the spinner to find the yarn ends quickly and easily. The skein should be bound loosely in at least two other places. For heavy skeins, weave the binding in and out—leave them loose, because the yarn will swell in water and the bindings could prevent penetration of water and dye. For storage, twist the skein and insert one loop inside the other (see page 36).

SETTING AND DISTRIBUTING THE TWIST

To set the twist and to even out twist distribution in spun yarn, the skeined yarn is wetted and weighted as it dries. This is not absolutely necessary, but it produces a more evenly twisted, controlled yarn. The skeins should be held taut—but not too taut—during drying. If they are stretched too much, the yarn will lose its elasticity. One method is to slip the wetted skeins over a rod and then suspend the rod. If the skeins are the same size, a second rod can go across the bottom and be weighted on each end. Otherwise, each skein can be weighted individually by tying a cord around the skein and attaching the weight to the cord. Many things can be used as weights—empty plastic bottles work well because they can be filled with just enough water to give the proper weight.

Z AND S TWIST AND PLYING

Throughout these instructions, frequent reference has been made to turning the spindle clockwise and to winding the yarn on to the spindle shaft clockwise. Obviously, the spindle could be turned in either direction and spinning would still occur. Once you start spinning in one direction, you must continue in that direction or you will merely untwist the yarn. Traditionally, and this holds true for today's machine-spun yarns, fibers are spun into yarn by turning the spindle to the right in a clockwise motion. This is called a Z twist. When two or more Z-twist yarns are plied or spun together, they are usually spun in the opposite direction, with

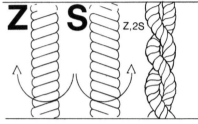

Direction of twist. Spun yarns have either a Z twist, which means they were spun by turning the spindle clockwise (to the right) or an S twist, counterclockwise (to the left). Most single yarns are spun with a Z twist. When two or more Z-twist yarns are spun or plied together, the spindle on to which they are spun is usually turned in a counterclockwise direction (S twist). This produces a yarn with balanced twist. "S" and "Z" are used as designations because the slanting bar in each letter corresponds to the angle that the twist in the yarn takes. The designation Z, 2 S indicates that the original twist was Z and then two such yarns were spun together, or plied, with an S twist.

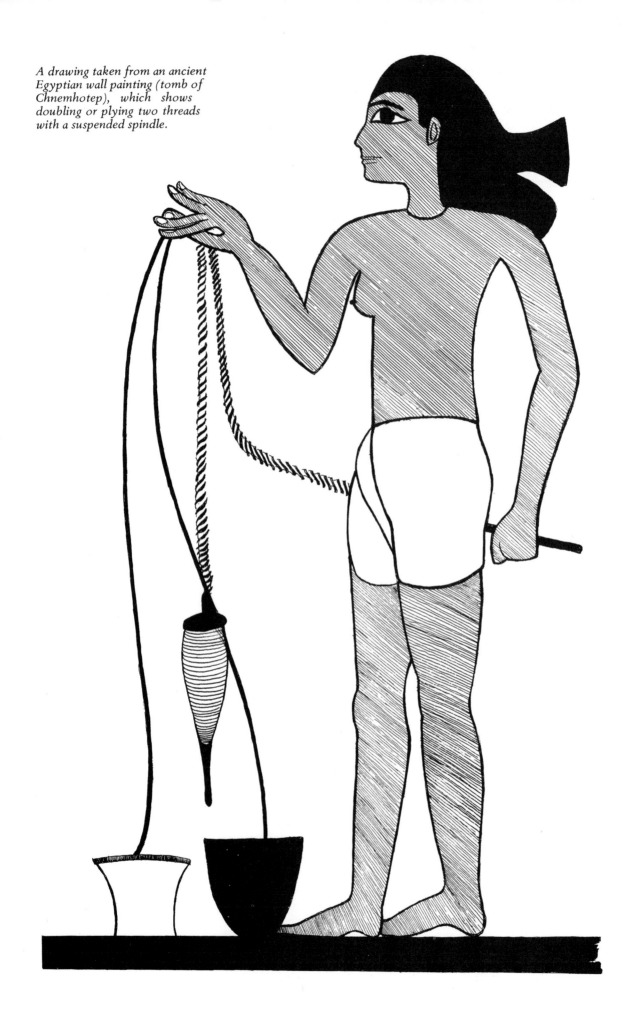

A drawing taken from an ancient Egyptian wall painting (tomb of Chnemhotep), which shows doubling or plying two threads with a suspended spindle.

The importance of spinning can be seen in ancient Peruvian gauze weaves. They are transparent, but also strong and resilient. A hard twist compensates for the fineness of the single-ply yarns and makes plying unnecessary. The overtwist gives a lively elasticity to the fabric and helps to hold the weft threads in place. Within a cloth, there will be yarns with different numbers of twists per inch, depending on the strength needed and the contrast desired for the pattern. Single yarns spun with an S or Z twist are also found within a single fabric. The differing twist direction influences the surface appearance giving a more pebbly effect.

a counterclockwise motion to the spindle (turned to the left to produce an S twist). Two or more single yarns spun in one direction will naturally go together if plied in the opposite direction. Single yarns destined for plying are usually spun fine with an overtwist, because, in the plying process (where the twist is reversed), some of the original twist is lost. Different yarn structures can be produced by combining many strands and using opposing twists. Yarns are plied for strength, for weight, or for bulk, to equalize the twist (especially for knitting or crocheting yarns) and for decorative and structural effects. Further decorative variations possible by plying, and spinner

control of the threads, are further discussed in Chapter 4.

The simplest method of plying is to wind the yarn into balls, drop the balls into baskets, pull out the ends, knot them to the starting cord, and, turning the spindle in the opposite (usually counterclockwise) direction, spin the yarns together. Any kind of spindle suspended or supported in any of the ways discussed can be used, although a heavy spindle is most often used because the additional weight is needed to get up the necessary momentum for the heavier yarn. It is also possible to wind the individual yarns—unplied—together into one big ball.

CHAPTER THREE

The Spinning Wheel

Is the wheel a marguerite, a daisy chain, the band?
Surely this tiny thing so sweet comes from Titania's Land.
Fairy workers must have shorn the cloudy fleeces white,
Or dandelions dainty puff when drift in lazy dreams,
Or spikey thistles downy fluff tumbling in sunny beams
Before the rosy glow of dawn put whimsy to flight.
They say a fairy has no heart, but sorrow now they feel
For mortal souls who grieve apart and so they've lent a wheel.
Spin little wheel a thread that is stout
Spin for our seamen true,
Spin the pain of parting out
From hearts which sorrow and rue.
   Spin the warmth of wool little wheel
   Forget your fairy days—
   Spin for the men so brave and leal
   Who guard the ocean ways.

The Fairy Wheel
Anonymous Poem from England

In the not too distant past, the spinning wheel was an important part of every household. It was frequently part of a woman's dowry, and, for many immigrants to North America, it was the only piece of furniture brought from the old country. A necessity, yes, but also an essential element of life that somehow brought rest and peace. The particular rhythm and feel of slowly treadling and feeding the fibers into the spindle orifice as they move and twist is an experience that is still available and special. This illustration is from an engraving by William Hincks. It shows the spinning and reeling of flax in County Down, Ireland, in 1783. Two spinners sit at their wheels, spinning flax from distaffs. The woman on the right is reeling spun thread into a skein from a full bobbin. Both wool and flax were spun in early Ireland, but England discouraged the wool industry in all her colonies, and, by the late eighteenth century, flax was the main fiber in use there. The resulting cottage industry was the foundation of the famous Irish linen.

The hand spindle is easily constructed and is portable. It can produce a beautiful, perfectly controlled yarn, but spinning large quantities of yarn takes a great deal of time. The spinning wheel can produce much more yarn in less time and with less effort. After learning how to spin on the drop spindle, most spinners are anxious to try the spinning wheel. This tool can be simple or complex, and, like the hand spindle, comes in many shapes and sizes.

All spinning wheels incorporate two basic components: a large drive wheel and a horizontally mounted spindle with a whorl that acts as a pulley. A spinning wheel can be crude and makeshift, or finely crafted with carefully balanced parts. Understanding the nature of the tool and how it functions is the key to successful spinning. This chapter will trace the development of the spinning wheel, explaining its various parts and their functions.

THE EARLY WHEEL

It is thought that the first development in the spinning wheel took place in India during the early Middle Ages. As with other crafts, textile work had achieved a very high level of preindustrial sophistication. Fine, highly skilled cotton spindle spinning had been going on for some 3,000 years, and Indian muslins were famous and highly sought after trade items. It was here that a spinning wheel was first used extensively over a geographically large area for spinning short fibers (cotton) into thread. This early wheel, sometimes referred to as the East Asian wheel or charka, was a logical extension of the hand spindle. The spindle was placed between two upright posts so the point extended out toward the spinner, parallel to the ground. The spindle whorl became a pulley, and a band traveled around it to a large drive wheel. The spinner sat on the ground or on a small stool, turning the wheel with one hand and drawing out the fibers with the other. This wheel, basically unchanged, is still in use throughout Asia.

THE SPINNING WHEEL IN EUROPE

The East Asian spinning wheel found its way to Europe, possibly

Perhaps one of the facets of spinning which recurs over and over again is the sheep-to-coat contest. This is frequently done at county fairs or sheep shearing events. One such account comes from England in 1811 concerning a bet made by John Throckmorton that wool could be obtained in the morning and a coat made from that wool worn to dinner that evening. The wager was for 1000 guineas. At 5 in the morning two sheep were brought in. The fleece were shorn, the fibers spun, the yarn woven, the cloth dyed, dried, and finished by 4 o'clock in the afternoon. The tailor then took the cloth and completed the coat by 6:20 and Sir John wore the coat to a special banquet he gave that evening for his friends in celebration of his winning his wager. The event was witnessed by over 5,000 people during which the shorn sheep were roasted and consumed along with 120 gallons of beer. It was later made the subject of a painting by Luke Clint.

This contemporary spinning wheel—called a Pakistani spinner, or Punjabi wheel—is basically the same design as the original East Asian wheel, with a large drive wheel and horizontal spindle quill. The spinner squats, sometimes on a low stool, and spins off the spindle tip while rotating the wheel by hand. The wheel is made of two large wood discs, joined in the center by a wooden axle hub and around the outer edge by a string or cord that zigzags the 4" across from one slotted disk-edge to the other. The drive band rests on the zigzag web and drives the spindle. The wheel is decorated with mirrors and shiny metallic pieces that reflect light as the wheel turns. Bells attached to the inner axle hub give sound to the motion.

An old spinning wheel from Afghanistan. The principle of its movement is the same as that of the Pakistani wheel. This wheel is light, graceful, and turns easily.

This drawing, taken from a fourteenth-century manuscript, illustrates the medieval European adaptation of the East Asian wheel.

brought by the Arabs, and was in use there by the late Middle Ages. Manuscript illustrations from that period show the European version. The wheel is mounted on legs so the spinner does not sit, but stands while working. In northern Europe, wool with longer, coarser fibers was spun on the wheel. Thus, under the European influence, the wheel grew larger and more stately. This spinning wheel, which we know today as the high wheel, was brought to the New World by colonists from the British Isles. In England, it has been called either the high or Jersey wheel; in Ireland, the long wheel; in Wales, the great wheel; and in Scotland, the Muckle wheel. In addition, it is sometimes called the wool wheel, because that fiber was traditionally spun on it,

and the walking wheel, because the spinner stands and walks back and forth, drawing out the fibers with one hand while the other hand controls the wheel.

QUILL WHEELS

The East Asian wheel and the walking wheel are early basic wheels. In both, the projecting spindle shaft is called a quill, and spinning is done off the tip of this rapidly revolving quill. Each time the spindle makes one rotation, one twist is inserted into the forming thread. As the difference between the diameter of the spindle pulley and the diameter of the drive wheel increases, the ratio of spindle turns per drive wheel revolution increases proportionately. Note that turning the drive wheel is a much more

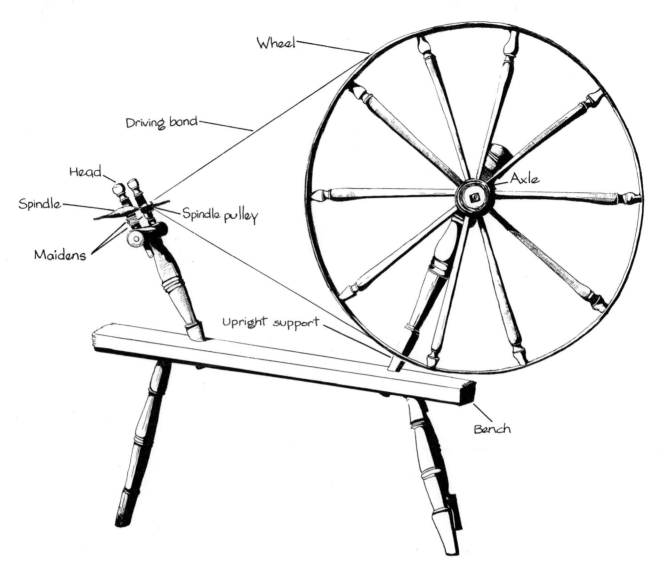

Wheel

Driving band

Head

Spindle

Spindle pulley

Maidens

Axle

Upright support

Bench

efficient use of energy than is turning the spindle by hand. The walking wheel usually comes with a tensioning device for shifting the spindle, so the drive band can be tightened or loosened.

American walking wheels are frequently equipped with an accelerating head, which is a second wheel mounted near the spindle. This wheel has two pulleys, a small pulley that receives the drive band from the large drive wheel, and a larger pulley, which, with a second, smaller belt, drives the spindle. This two-pulley arrangement multiplies or accelerates the number of revolutions turned by the spindle; this system was widely adopted, and is now found in many kinds of spinning wheels. Its main drawback is that it creates a second drive

band, and requires a second tensioning device for fine adjustment. The outstanding advantage of the quill type wheel is its simplicity and directness—the yarn does not have to go through any holes. If it is hairy or kinky, it will still wind on to the spindle. This kind of wheel has an inherent slowness, because the yarn is first spun and then the hand shifted, allowing the spun yarn to wind on to the spindle shaft.

There are also wheels that are designed not for spinning, but for use as bobbin winders. Wound bobbins, sometimes and rather confusingly referred to as quills, are inserted into shuttles, which carry the weft thread back and forth in loom weaving. This kind of wheel, also called a quill winder, has either

The European wheel shown in the previous illustration eventually developed into a large, graceful wheel for spinning wool. This kind of wheel is frequently called a high, wool, or walking wheel. The projecting spindle and the large drive wheel, which measures 5 to 6 feet in diameter, are its most obvious characteristics. Most of these wheels have three legs and a tension device that shifts the spindle for controlling the drive band tension. The wheel is turned by hand, and the spinner steps back and forth as she spins. An experienced spinner might walk twenty miles in a day's work.

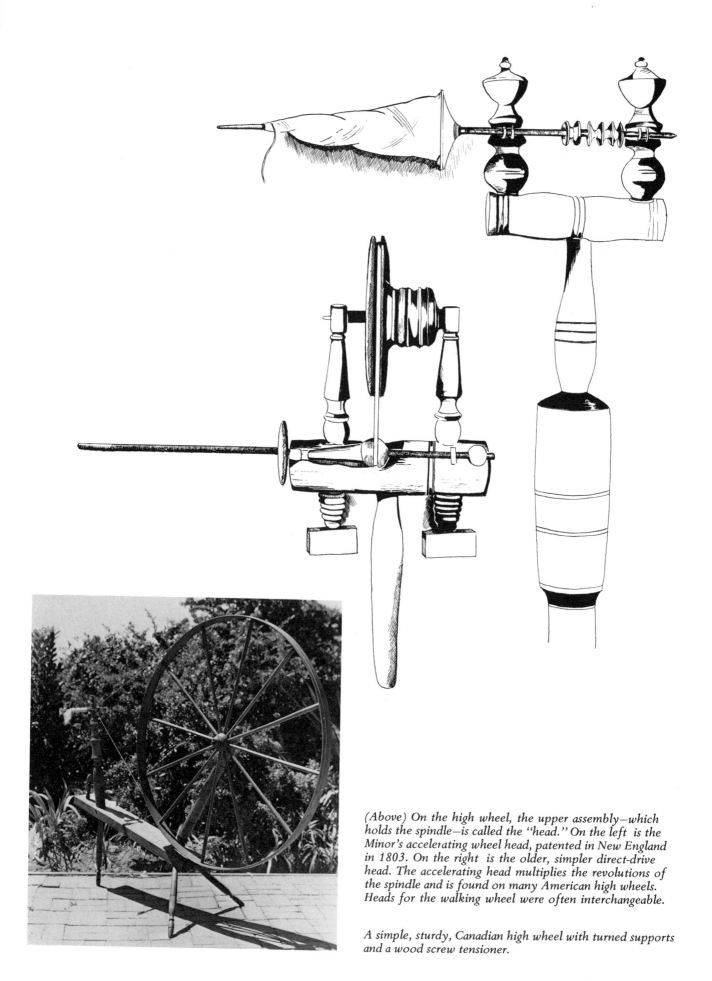

(Above) On the high wheel, the upper assembly—which holds the spindle—is called the "head." On the left is the Minor's accelerating wheel head, patented in New England in 1803. On the right is the older, simpler direct-drive head. The accelerating head multiplies the revolutions of the spindle and is found on many American high wheels. Heads for the walking wheel were often interchangeable.

A simple, sturdy, Canadian high wheel with turned supports and a wood screw tensioner.

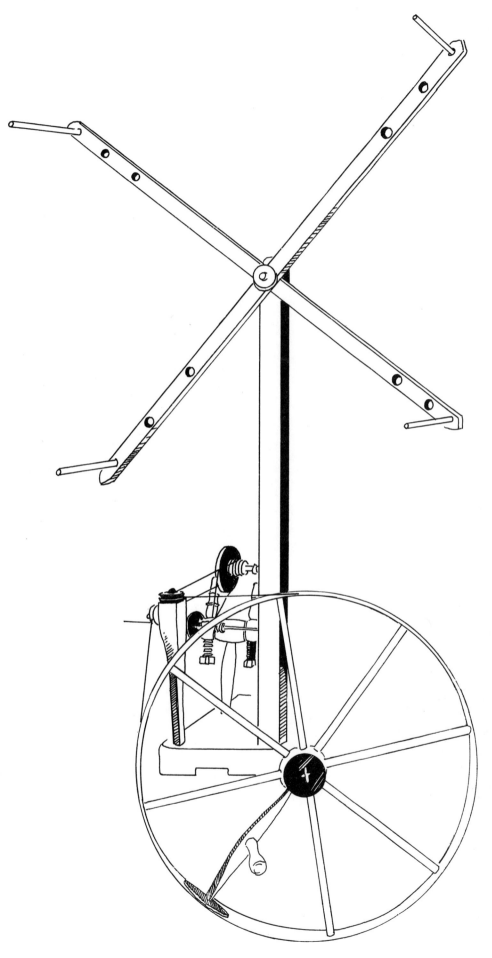

This wheel is an interesting adaptation of the high wheel. It was patented by a man named Hathorn, from Maine, in the late nineteenth century. This ingenious and compact design, which clamps to a table corner, provides the spinner with a reel, a swift, and a bobbin winder in addition to the basic spinning device. The drive band goes from the large wheel around the corner to an accelerating head. The four-armed reel has movable pegs for making larger or smaller skeins. The reel can be made to lie flat on the spinning wheel table, where it is used as a swift for holding the skeined yarn after washing or dyeing. The spindle is also used to wind bobbins for weaving.

a thick, blunt spindle or no spindle at all, but just a rod between two widely spaced maidens (spindle supports). Quilltype spinning wheels, incidentally, may be used as bobbin winders.

Quilltype wheels are used occasionally for demonstrations, but most modern handspinners prefer more sophisticated, higher production wheels. Two very useful contemporary adaptations of the quill concept are shown on pages 48 and 49. The wheel on page 49 was designed for the use of weaving students at San Francisco State University, where it is used to spin heavy, bulky yarns that would snag

> The charka is, above all, the wheel of knowledge and wisdom, peace and tranquility. It restrains passions and gives repose to the senses; it restores calm to the troubled mind. In short, it is the panacea for a hundred ills, the elixir of life and the philosopher's stone.
>
> Pattabhi Sitaramayya

on anything but a simple quill. Everything about it is heavy and sturdy to accommodate thick, relatively inflexible fibers. The wheel incorporates a treadle, so the spinner sits and turns the wheel by foot power, leaving both hands free to deal with the fibers.

The wheel on page 49 was designed for portability and low cost, and has the ability to spin a fine, tight cotton thread. The parts are compact and lightweight, and all tension devices are made from springs. It folds into a small suitcase with a handle and is called a charka. Its use was encouraged by Gandhi as a means of achieving economic independence and peace of mind. Gandhi frequently spun on this

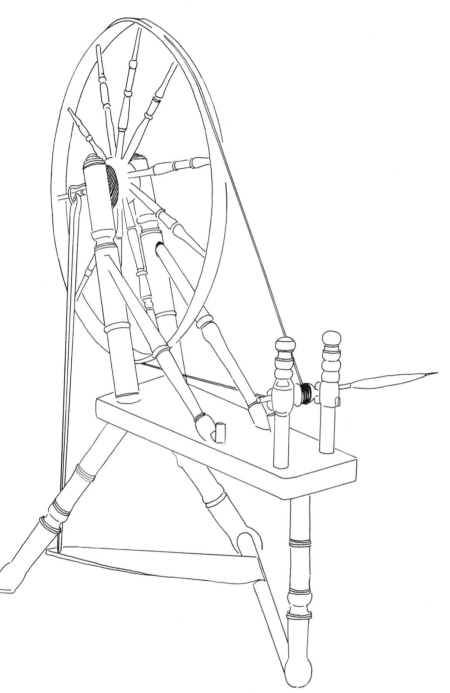

This nineteenth-century quill, or spindle, wheel from eastern Canada is another adaptation of the high wheel. There is no tension device for tightening the drive band, but the wheel has a treadle that is worked by foot, leaving both hands free to control the fibers.

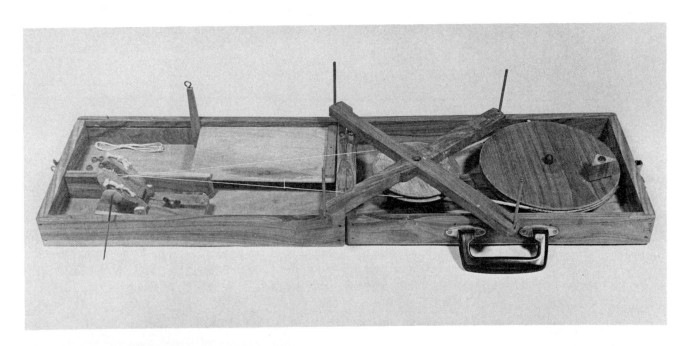

(Above) This contemporary East Asian wheel was developed when Gandhi was the Hindu Nationalist leader. It became his symbol and is frequently referred to as Gandhi's charka. He felt that spinning was good for the soul and that it was also the key to economic independence. Through competitions, he encouraged the design of a small wheel that was light, easily assembled, and inexpensive. It is specifically designed for spinning cotton, a fiber common throughout India. This version of the Gandhi charka folds into a small suitcase and weighs less than six pounds. This wheel is shown in the photograph open and ready for use—the reel, which is shown in position, is removed during spinning (the parts fit in the space under the drive wheels). Although the wheel is crude, it is easy and effortless to work. Tension is created by springs. The accelerating principle is used to keep the drive wheel small but effective. The big wheel on the right is turned by hand. The power is transmitted through wheels and pulleys to the spindle, which revolves many times for each turn of the hand-driven wheel. When the charka is folded up, the small parts (spindles, drive bands, and so on) go into a built-in compartment that has a sliding lid. A small slat with an eye turns up from the compartment and acts as a guide for the spun yarn during reeling.

This compact contemporary quill wheel, designed by Alden Amos, is made for spinning heavy, hard-to-manage yarns. This vertically arranged wheel is especially sturdy. The small drive wheel turns easily on bearings, and the angle of the quill can be shifted for comfort.

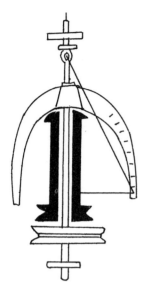

A cut-away view of the bobbin in position on the spindle. The bobbin is a loose element frequently removed for reeling yarn, and it must slide easily on and off the spindle. The bobbin is removed by slipping the drive band off the pulleys and unscrewing the spindle pulley. Spindle pulleys sometimes have two drive band grooves, or channels, of varying diameters. When the drive belt is placed in the groove with the larger diameter, the spindle rotates less and produces a lightly twisted yarn, while placing the belt in the smaller diameter groove gives more twist and a firmer yarn.

kind of wheel, and encouraged all Indians to use it.

THE BOBBIN AND FLYER ASSEMBLY

In Europe, the late Middle Ages brought two improvements in the spinning wheel: the treadle and the bobbin-flyer assembly. With the treadle, a wheel could be turned by foot, leaving both hands free to control the fibers. Spinning on the quill wheel was intermittent—the twisting of the fibers had to be interrupted every few feet so the yarn could be wound on to the spindle. The addition of the treadle was a logical step and made the wheel much faster, but spinning was still intermittent. The bobbin-flyer assembly, on the other hand, was a truly remarkable and sophisticated development. It allowed for simultaneously twisting the fibers and winding the newly spun yarn. This invention is generally credited to a German, Johann Jürgen, who developed it in 1530. Earlier drawings by Leonardo da Vinci show a similar mechanism, but Jurgen actually made and used the device for spinning.

The flyer mechanism remains basically unchanged—it is shown in the illustrations on page 50.

The spindle tip is the orifice through which the newly spun thread passes. The flyer is a two-armed, U-shaped mechanism, fitted with hooks that help distribute the spun fibers evenly over the bobbin. The spindle and flyer are integral parts and move at the same rate. The spindle whorl is still a pulley, but it screws loose from the spindle, allowing a bobbin to slide on to the spindle shaft to rest within the U of the flyer. The bobbin has a smaller pulley that rests next to the spindle pulley. The spun thread passes through the orifice at the end of the spindle closest to the spinner and out through a second opening just before the point at which the base of the U of the flyer attaches to the spindle. The spun thread emerges from the hollow portion of the spindle and is wrapped neatly on to the bobbin, guided into place by the hooks on the flyer arms. A single drive band is doubled around the large drive wheel; one loop passes over the

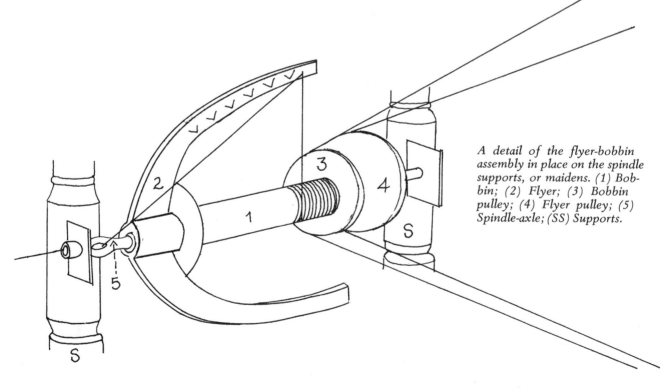

A detail of the flyer-bobbin assembly in place on the spindle supports, or maidens. (1) Bobbin; (2) Flyer; (3) Bobbin pulley; (4) Flyer pulley; (5) Spindle-axle; (SS) Supports.

The Saxony style wheel has a drive wheel off to the right, the mother-of-all with bobbin and flyer to the left, a treadle under the usually slanted table, and three legs. Most spinning wheels with a flyer and bobbin have similar parts, even though their arrangement might be different. The wheel shown is late nineteenth century French Canadian, designed for spinning wool. The large drive wheel (larger than on many Saxony wheels) is responsible for this wheel's steady, high-speed performance. The frame is light but sturdy, with a large and finely balanced flyer. A very light, sensitive treadle offers no hesitation, and the action is very fast.

Parts of the Saxony wheel shown are: (A) Wheel; (B) Drive band; (C) Bobbin; (D) Flyer; (E) Leather bearings; (F) Maidens (spindle supports); (G) Mother-of-all; (H) Tension screw; (I) Table; (J) Uprights (wheel supports); (K) Treadle; (L) Treadle bar; (M) Treadle cord; (N) Footman; (O) Axle crank.

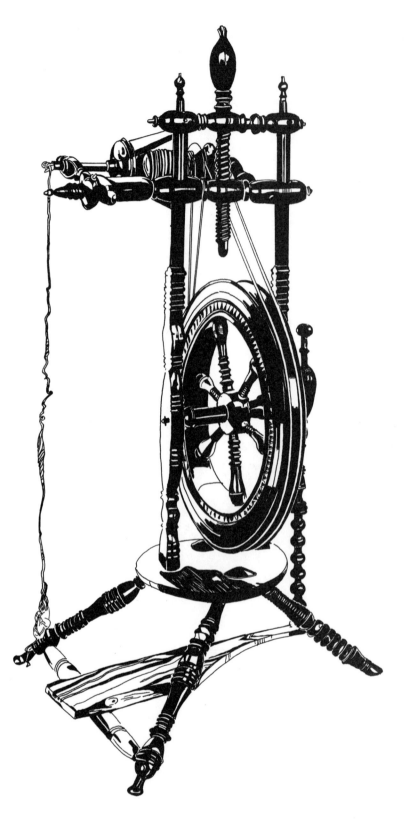

This highly finished German wheel is a variation on the horizontally arranged Saxony wheel. This type, where the drive wheel is under the flyer-bobbin assembly, is usually called a castle, or parlor, wheel. It has the advantage of taking up very little space, but the smaller drive wheel requires more treadling. Castle wheels are not good production wheels because of their small size and lightness, but they are excellent traveling companions.

spindle pulley, and the other loop passes over the bobbin pulley. As the spinner treadles, the twist is inserted by the flyer-spindle as it rotates and as the spun thread is drawn around the bobbin. Since the bobbin pulley is smaller than the flyer pulley, the bobbin revolves more rapidly than the flyer, which in turn draws the thread in and around the bobbin. As the foot treadles and the drive wheel turns, spinning and winding continue simultaneously.

This kind of wheel, shown on page 51, is usually called a Brunswick, or Saxony, wheel, after Johan Jürgen's home area. The majority of these wheels made in the seventeenth and eighteenth centuries were used for spinning flax. Small orifices, tiny hooks, and a distaff are characteristic of the spinning wheels of flax spinners. Traditionally, wool was spun on the high wheel and flax on the Saxony, or low, wheel. Most wheels of this style that are made today have larger bobbins, flyers, hooks, and orifices, so they can be used for heavier yarns as well. They are primarily designed to spin and accommodate medium-weight wool yarns.

The illustrations on pages 50 and 51 show the basic parts of a Saxony wheel. The tension screw shifts the mother-of-all to loosen or tighten the drive band. The bobbin-flyer assembly is usually held in position on the maidens by leather bearings, and one of the maidens usually twists to release the flyer assembly. The wheel shown has a tiny pin, like a toothpick, that holds the leather bearing in position; when it is removed, the leather slides out of the maiden and releases the spindle.

When the double drive band is tensioned, the adjustment for both the bobbin pulley and the flyer-

A contemporary Norwegian wheel with the same fast action as the Canadian wheel. It has a built-in holder under the mother-of-all for storing extra bobbins. The baskets are a functional addition for holding balls of yarn during plying. The flat table, characteristic of traditional Norwegian wheels, is a convenient tray.

Contemporary spinning wheel from New Zealand, with a metal-weighted drive wheel. It has an interesting tension device—as the round wood knob on the upper right is turned, the flyer moves up or down, increasing or decreasing tension. Extra bobbins rest on pegs at the center.

A contemporary American wheel with functional simplicity. The bobbin and flyer are released by twisting the back maiden, which has a long peg that gives the hand leverage. The general sturdiness of the wheel adds weight, which gives it an especially steady feel. Heavier wheels are best for spinning up heavier yarns. A considerable quantity of yarn can be built up on this extra-large bobbin before winding off becomes necessary. The three-legged stool was especially designed for the owner of the wheel.

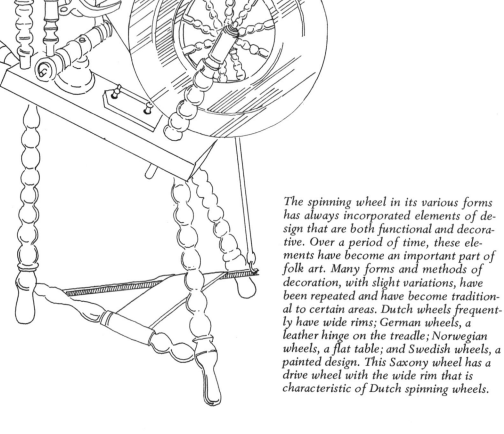

The spinning wheel in its various forms has always incorporated elements of design that are both functional and decorative. Over a period of time, these elements have become an important part of folk art. Many forms and methods of decoration, with slight variations, have been repeated and have become traditional to certain areas. Dutch wheels frequently have wide rims; German wheels, a leather hinge on the treadle; Norwegian wheels, a flat table; and Swedish wheels, a painted design. This Saxony wheel has a drive wheel with the wide rim that is characteristic of Dutch spinning wheels.

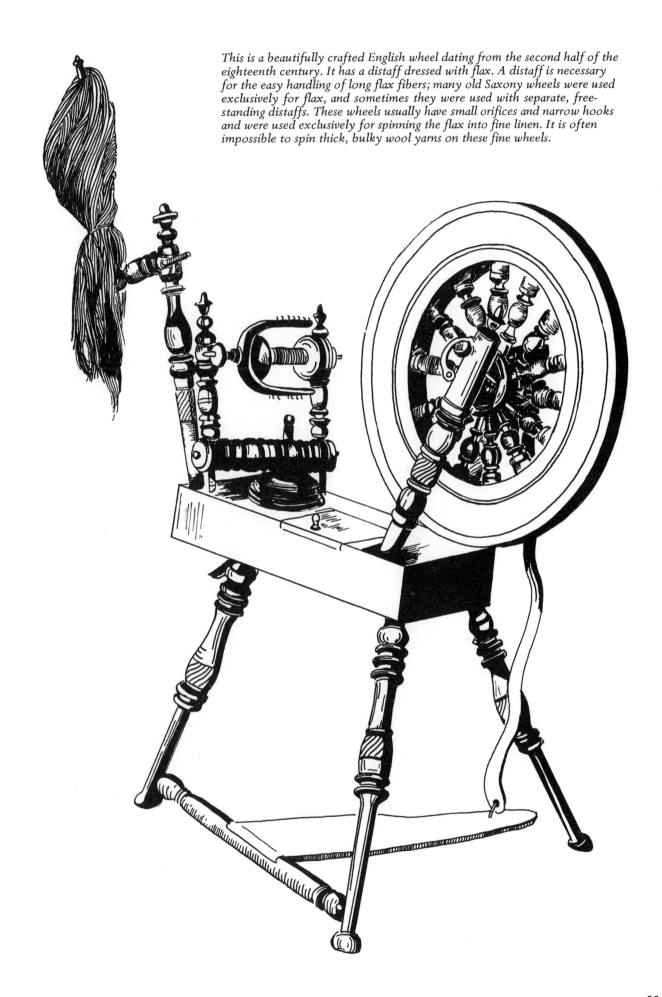

This is a beautifully crafted English wheel dating from the second half of the eighteenth century. It has a distaff dressed with flax. A distaff is necessary for the easy handling of long flax fibers; many old Saxony wheels were used exclusively for flax, and sometimes they were used with separate, free-standing distaffs. These wheels usually have small orifices and narrow hooks and were used exclusively for spinning the flax into fine linen. It is often impossible to spin thick, bulky wool yarns on these fine wheels.

A modern castle wheel with a built-in bobbin holder that can be used for plying yarns. The thick-rimmed wheel gives stability and momentum. Like most contemporary spinning wheels, it has a flyer and orifice that will accommodate medium-weight wool yarns.

This castle wheel, which has four legs rather than three and looks as though it might have been constructed from erector set parts, is made almost entirely of metal, and is lightweight and open. Called a Columbine, it is a good, smooth spinner and travels well. The foot treadle, big enough for both feet, has a nonsliding surface. It is painted bright orange and comes with either a small or large orifice. Despite its fragile appearance, this castle wheel is exceptionally stable.

A wooden model of a simple, sturdy seventeenth-century wheel. It is an early example of a flyer wheel with a single drive band.

spindle pulley occurs simultaneously. Slippage of belts and bands on pulleys and wheels can sometimes occur from over or undertension, or from misalignment. Slippage can be controlled by the experienced spinner to regulate the amount of twist and the rate of winding by varying the amount of resistance in his or her pull.

THE FLYER WITH A SINGLE DRIVE BAND

The bobbin-flyer assembly previously described used a double drive band, but it can also be arranged to use a single drive band, turning either the flyer-spindle pulley or the bobbin pulley. The Ashford wheel shown on page 58 is an example of such a wheel. It has what is called a flyer lead—only the flyer, which inserts twist, is driven. There is a brake, sometimes called a Scotch tension, mounted on the mother-of-all, and this brake puts

tension on the bobbin. This brake is made of a length of monofilament and a rubber band and goes over the bobbin pulley. It is tightened just enough to pull the bobbin against the spindle, causing it to turn, and, consequently, to pull in the thread so it winds on to the bobbin. This adjustment is critical. If it's just a bit off, spinning will be difficult. The elasticity of the rubber band gives enough play so the tension does not continually work loose.

If the single drive band goes to the bobbin pulley, the wheel has a bobbin lead. As the drive wheel turns, rotating the bobbin, the spun thread is drawn around the bobbin. The flyer and spindle are turned by the drag of the thread on the flyer hooks. Bobbin lead wheels usually have a brake that puts a drag on the flyer-spindle; but this brake is not necessary, and spinning can easily be done without its use.

The Ashford wheel from New Zealand is very popular today. It is an inexpensive, sturdy wheel designed after World War II to encourage home spinning in New Zealand; it comes in kit form. The Ashford spinner was designed to spin wool knitting yarns, soft yarns with a low amount of twist. Many spinning suppliers make special attachments for this wheel: distaffs, heads, smaller diameter pulleys, and quills. The single drive band turns the flyer, and the bobbin pulley has a brake (sometimes called a scotch tension) controlled by the knob on the left. A second knob under the flyer turns to lift the mother-of-all up or down, controlling tension on the drive band. The wheel comes with three extra bobbins and a separate holder, called a lazy kate.

This is a box, or chair, wheel with four legs, a large orifice, and an oversize bobbin and flyer assembly. It is called an Indian Spinner because similar heads were used by North Coast Indians in Canada to spin bulky yarns for sweaters. This kind of wheel is sometimes called the wolf, because it "eats" sheep's wool at a rapid rate. The oak-bodied Indian Spinner shown uses an old barrow wheel, which adds weight, helps sustain momentum, and gives a nice smooth action. This wheel is primarily designed to spin bulky, low-twist yarns. The leather drive band turns the bobbin, causing the thread to drag on the flyer hook, which turns the flyer, creating the spin. At the front of the wheel, above the orifice, is a brake designed to put a drag on the flyer. There is no tension device for the drive band, so the leather band must be lengthened or shortened to change the tension. (Photograph by David Donoho.)

This wheel incorporates a similar head with the large flyer and bobbin drive. The entire lower portion is from an old treadle sewing machine. The spinner sits in front of the treadle, and the yarn feeds into the orifice from the side. Old treadle sewing machines were designed for smooth, easy treadling, and they adapt well to the Indian Spinner head.

59

This electric spinning wheel does away with treadling. It is made from parts of an electric sewing machine. It is compact and can be set up on a tray or table. The foot pedal controls the speed, and lead weights slipped on to a hook near the motor control the tension on the drive band. This particular model has an extra-large orifice and over-sized hooks. There is a brake on the bobbin.

In the examples shown, the brake goes over the spindle near the front orifice. Many spinners prefer the single drive band and feel that it offers them greater control over the spinning process.

THE ELECTRIC SPINNER

The electric spinner really belongs in a class or category outside the traditional handspinning apparatus. The electric spinner, however, shares many characteristics with the traditional wheels. When well designed, the electric spinner can be fast, smooth, efficient, and easily controlled. The rate of spindle rotation is determined usually by a foot pedal of the sort used on electric sewing machines, or, less often, by a rheostat like those sometimes used to dim electric lights. The electric spinner shown above is compact, efficient, and a pleasure to spin on. This wheel represents a logical modern development in handspinning. It is not designed for industry, but for the modern handspinner who needs or appreciates this wedding of new and old. The spinner still controls the fibers, the speed of the machine, and all the adjustments, but he or she no longer has to treadle.

For many spinners, this wheel seems impure and somehow improper, and offers little pleasure, but there are some distinct advantages. Since the wheel is driven by electricity and not by foot, the drive wheel can be small and the entire arrangement very compact.

This particular machine uses Jürgens bobbin-flyer assembly and is capable of producing the same yarns that would come from a similarly set up treadle wheel. The only real difference is that the wheel is driven by electric rather than human power. Any kind of spinning wheel or spinning wheel head could be adapted to being electrically driven.

A HISTORY OF THE SPINNING WHEEL

Although the wheel showed little change between the sixteenth and nineteenth centuries, many types and designs developed that show marked differences. During this period in Europe and after 1620 in Colonial America, the spinning wheel was an integral part of family life. As people prospered, their wheels became fancier and more special. Although wheels were made for everyday use, special highly decorated and delicate ones with ivory finials, complicated turnings, and bone bearings were also built—especially in Europe. These so-called parlor wheels were for occasional spinning and were sometimes more decorative than functional. In Colonial America, life was harder and simpler than in Europe. The relative austerity of American wheel design was also influenced by the severity of religious belief. The Shakers especially designed and manufactured many high wheels and Saxony wheels during the late eighteenth and nineteenth centuries. Generally speaking, spinning wheels were sturdier and simpler in America.

Like their counterparts elsewhere, American women spent time whenever they could find it preparing fibers and spinning on their wheels. Spinning times were often very social, since all ages were involved in some phase of fiber preparation. Most of the jobs involved—and this is especially true of spinning—kept the workers busy but allowed them to chat, gossip, and converse freely.

In Colonial America, spinning bees and competitions were encouraged, and women took pride in the quality and quantity of yarn produced. These events were social occasions for getting the spinning done. Long days and evenings of community spinning often ended with good food, singing, and dancing. Spinning and the production of flax and wool were clear-cut means of gaining political and economic independence. The word homespun took on patriotic implications, and

Cross-patch
Draw the latch,
Sit by the fire and spin;
Take a cup
And drink it up,
Then call your neighbors in.

Anonymous Rhyme

the Harvard College class of 1768 and the Yale class of 1769 elected to wear only clothing made from homespun for their graduation ceremonies. The spinning room at Mt. Vernon, Washington's home, is still filled with Saxony wheels for spinning flax and high wheels for spinning wool.

The spinning wheel has always been a symbol of feminene virtue and industry. It was familiar to the rich and to the poor. An excerpt from a letter from Benjamin Franklin to his sister, dated January 6, 1736, indicates his adherence to this widely held belief:

I had almost determined on a tea-table; but when I considered that the character of a good housewife was far preferable to that of only being a pretty gentlewoman, I concluded to send you a spinning-wheel.

Two hundred and fifty years after Johann Jürgen developed the flyer and bobbin, Richard Arkwright came up with the idea of a moving bobbin, the principle of which is used on modern spinning machines. As the industrial revolution moved rapidly ahead, the ubiquitous spinning wheel came to be less and less common. As the power machinery took over and the wheels retired to the attic, preindustrial life began to disappear too. These words from an old man reflected a common feeling:

> When t'ould wheels died out, the gude times went too, m'happen they's come back if t'wheels did.

Today there is a new awareness of crafts and textiles, and spinning wheels are being retrieved from the attics and antique stores not so much for decoration as for spinning. People are using wheels again and adapting them to contemporary needs. New wheels are being designed and manufactured because more and more people want to spin.

CHOOSING A WHEEL

There are many factors to consider when choosing a wheel, including your reasons for spinning and the kind of yarn to be produced. Some people spin because they like the tools; some because they want to work the yarn; some to produce yarn for market; many spin to achieve peace of mind; and other spin for the pure joy of spinning. Certain yarns cannot be readily purchased, so sometimes handweavers or knitters will spin their own yarn because they have no other choice. Many other factors might influence one's choice of wheel, and many spinners find that once they begin, their needs and tastes change.

Some general rules for choosing a wheel are: all moving parts should work with ease; the drive wheel should line up with the spindle pulley and not be warped or off center; all parts should be intact and the wood in good condition. It is easiest to spin a fine, controlled yarn on a light wheel with a small orifice. Bulky, textured yarns require a heavy wheel with a large orifice and bobbin. If you want to spin especially inflexible fibers or overspun yarns, a sturdy quill-type wheel with nothing to interfere with the thread might be the best answer.

If you like to cart your wheel around or you have limited space, a vertical castle wheel might meet your needs best. A large Saxony wheel that requires a minimum of treadling, with a fast spin and take in, is the best production wheel—unless you want to try the electric spinner. For bulkier yarns, the stability of a chair, or box, wheel (Indian Spinner) with an oversize bobbin is very satisfactory.

New wheels are widely available and should be purchased only if you are adequately pleased by the size, shape, appearance, action, and price of the instrument—look around before making a decision. Check through recent issues of weaving magazines (listed at the back of the book), and send away for brochures. Spin on different wheels, talk to experienced spinners, and then do what seems reasonable. Generally speaking, more expensive wheels will be made of hardwood, have more turned parts, and show better craftsmanship and more individual care in construction. Unless you are an experienced spinner, don't buy a wheel from someone who does not spin until you are sure that it functions properly. There are many wheels, both new and old, that were not made for spinning.

Not everyone agrees, but many spinners feel that there is some very special pleasure that comes from spinning on an old wheel. An old wheel often comes from some rare source, an ancestor, a friend, or some unusual place where it was found unexpectedly, waiting to be brought home.

Antique wheels are sometimes found by chance, and, if you find one, you will probably have to make a very difficult, immediate decision. Generally, it is reasonable to follow the rule that if you like it and have the money, buy it. However, keep in mind that on many older wheels, parts are either missing, not original, or are badly chipped and cracked. Minor damage, if it does not interfere with the spinning, may be ignored. Look for signs of good and poor craftsmanship. European wheels frequently have worm damage, and wood can look perfect on the outside but be eaten away on the inside. The footman, treadle, legs, leather pieces, and supports can be easily replaced. But warped wheels and badly damaged heads can be expensive and tricky to repair or replace, since they require expert attention. Any major repair work on an antique wheel should be done by an experienced woodworker who specializes in spinning wheels. Whenever possible, seek the advice of someone more experienced than yourself when buying an antique wheel.

There are also interesting old wheels that turn up occasionally which are not especially practical but are fascinating. Among these are wheels with two heads, made so two yarns can be spun simultaneously; delicate little courting wheels, designed to go on a table—as the young maiden spun the thread, her suitor worked the treadle; and the pendulum wheel, a variation on the high wheel, in which the spinner sits near the floor and turns the large wheel with one hand while drawing the fibers with the other hand. The spindle is on an extension weighted at the top. When the treadle is depressed, the spindle moves away from the spinner; when the treadle is released, the weight at the top returns the spindle. Other types of wheels come with built-in reelers, special compartments inside the table, and built-in racks for bobbins. Occasionally, one sees a wheel with a double treadle, so both feet work.

In the very early American colonies, nearly everyone knew how to weave, and most people had been spinning since childhood. The women bore the greatest responsibility for the fashioning of fabric and clothing for the family, and they used every bit of the fleece or fiber available, with the normal "sad-colored" cloth being composed of "one-third white wool, one-third black sheep's wool, one-third scraps dyed with indigo." Sheep were protected and valued—they were seldom used for food and were allowed to graze freely. In the Connecticut colony in 1640, the General Court ordered that "every family within these plantations shall procure and plant at least one spoonfull of English hempe seed in fruitful soyle at least a foot distance betwixt each seed."

CARE AND ADJUSTMENT

All wheels are different and special. They must be treated with care and respect. Care for a spinning wheel in the same way you would any fine piece of wood furniture. Frequent lubrication of all moving parts, including any leather, is necessary for proper functioning. A lightweight oil should be used for fast-moving parts and grease for slow-moving parts.

In general, the points needing lubrication are: holes where metal pins hold the treadle bar to the front legs; the treadle cord; the axle and the slots the axle turns in; the top of the footman; the bearings on the maidens; the center metal shaft of the flyer; and the center of each bobbin. Both soap and paraffin are good for lubricating wooden parts and for eliminating squeaks.

Sometimes new spinning wheels, especially those that come in kit form, will arrive with the wood parts untreated. Some spinners prefer to leave them unfinished, allowing the natural oils of use to create a patina, but many others like a darker stained surface. Many different stains or wood finishes are available, and choice of color depends on individual preference—antique wheels are usually dark, and they are sometimes varnished or painted. Wood should be gone over with fine sandpaper or fine steel wool before any finish is applied. If you prefer the natural color of the wood, use a combination of beeswax and turpentine or a good quality floor wax to preserve it. Always be careful of the sensitive bobbin and flyer. And don't wax or polish the wheel edge, or the drive band will lose friction and slide when it should grip.

When in storage, spinning wheels should be left intact and not disassembled to prevent parts from getting lost, warped, or mixed up. Apparently identical parts are not necessarily interchangeable, and become less so with use. Also keep in mind that new wheels and wheels that have not been in use usually take a while to break in, and may take months of active treadling before they function perfectly.

On the traditional walking wheel—and sometimes on other kinds of wheels—many of the support parts are tapered to force fit. The drive wheel must be aligned with the spindle pulley or the drive band will slide off the rim. To adjust the high wheel, tap the wheel support under the table with a mallet to loosen it, and then shift the support so the wheel lines up. Turn the wheel with the drive band on to make sure it tracks properly. When you are satisfied, give a good solid tap to the support top to firmly lodge it in place. This last tap can throw it off, so perfect adjustment takes patience and practice. Some spindle pulleys have grooves, and the drive band can be shifted from one groove to another, providing a point of adjustment.

Drive bands should not stretch and should have friction to catch on the pulleys. Some wheels have wide pulley grooves and are designed for a leather band. Most wheels have narrow pulley grooves and require a cord. The cord should be a light twist cotton, with a thickness in proportion to the wheel to give the necessary friction without any stretching. Before mounting the cord, adjust the tension device at the halfway point or less, so the cord can be loosened or tightened.

The cord ends can be tied in a square knot or weavers' knot, but ideally they should be spliced. It is also possible to taper the ends and bind the join with sewing thread. A coating of beeswax or belt dressing will protect the cord and give it good friction. Leather bands are either stitched at the ends or held with a sturdy metal staple.

The arrangement of the drive band is either a single loop driving one pulley, or a single loop doubled driving the two pulleys. If the band is doubled, there will be a place where the cord crosses. If the treadle turns the wheel to the right (clockwise to produce a Z-twist yarn), the cross will be just under or to the left of the head. This is the usual arrangement. When the wheel is treadled counterclockwise, the direction usually used for plying, the cross will naturally shift or migrate to the top or right side of the head.

Once the wheel parts are smoothly functioning and the drive band is taut, further adjustments based entirely on tension are done during spinning. Getting used to a wheel, breaking it in, and learning how it works best are important parts of owning and enjoying a spinning wheel.

As with any tool, adjustments and changes can be made to meet the user's needs. A wheel with a double drive band can be converted to a single drive band by driving just one pulley and putting a brake consisting of a cord and rubber band over the other pulley.

The choice of brake anchoring point depends on the design of the spinning wheel. Pulley ratio can be changed by deepening or filling up pulley grooves. Distaffs can be added or taken away, and wheel rims can be weighted to stabilize the wheel and perpetuate momentum. Any flyer wheel can be made into a quill wheel by carefully wedging an appropriate size dowel into the front orifice.

The spinning wheel is a magical tool with beautiful moving parts. It has balance, motion, sound, and function. It is part of our tradition and heritage. Fibers are not only spun into yarn, but troubles are spun away and dreams are created.

Turn, keep turning, wheel of Fate,
Cease from spinning threads of grey
Colourless monotony
Spin me no drab
But spin me gay.
Blue for love and red for hate—
Purple grief, rich wine of eve,
Dusky twilight's symphony.
Yellow sunshine
Shades of day,
Harmony,
For the cloth that I shall weave.

Forward, forward, turn the wheel
To the shining years ahead,
Colour vendor
Spin me splendour
Cob-web tender,
For my loom and for my reel.
Shuttle flying with bright thread
To weave my cloth
Light as moth
Or champagne froth
To celebrate.
Onward turn, my wooden wheel,
True as finely tempered steel,
Wasting not a single shred.

Spinning Wheel
Anonymous Poem

CHAPTER FOUR

Spinning on the Wheel

Twinkle, twinkle, pretty spindle,
    Let the white wool drift and dwindle;
Oh! we weave a damask doublet
    For my love's coat of steel.
Hark! the timid turning treadle
    Crooning soft old-fashioned ditties,
To the low, slow murmur of the
    Brown, round wheel.

Old Irish Song

Spinning in progress.

Once you learn how to spin on the drop spindle and begin to more fully understand the characteristics and functions of the spinning wheel, actual spinning on the wheel should soon become easy and natural. There are no absolute rules to wheel spinning, but as with the hand spindle, there are principles and there are methods that lend themselves to greater speed and efficiency. The many photographs in this chapter are meant to give you a view of different styles and methods. With a little practice, you can learn to do any of them with ease.

There are many factors discussed in later chapters that might make you choose one method over another, including the length of the fibers; whether they are sticky, fine, coarse, well-prepared, or tangled; and the size and kind of yarn desired. This chapter concentrates on two methods of spinning—the short draw and the long draw. The short draw is slower but allows for more hand manipulation. It is best for fibers that have had little preparation and that have many variations in texture. It also works best for spinning thick yarns and for spinning long fibers. The short draw is easiest to learn, since your hands work in much the same way they do for the method of drop spindle spinning shown in Chapter 2. The long draw requires larger, more sweeping motions, and longer extensions of the arm. It works well with short fibers and with well-prepared fibers that will slide easily. It is fast, rhythmical, and with practice becomes smooth and easy. The two spinning methods are not mutually exclusive, and many spinners have a style that combines the two.

The basic principles of wheel spinning can be applied to any fiber. (Specific fiber characteristics and how they affect the spinning properties are further dealt with in the fiber chapters.) As with spindle spinning, it is recommended that you begin on the wheel with sheep's wool of medium length (3 to 5") and medium grade. It should be relatively clean, but need not be washed. Wool fleece from New Zealand, which is invariably clean, with a nice feel, is easy to learn with, and is perfect for the beginner. It or an equivalent is available from any general spinning supplier.

If wheel spinning feels very awkward at first, or if you want a smoother, more controlled yarn and fibers that draw more easily, read through the next chapter on fiber preparation, and then come back to the wheel. Some spinners spend considerable time and attention on fiber preparation before spinning on the wheel, while others spend none at all. The amount of preparation necessary depends on the fibers, the kind of yarn control desired, and how you want the yarn to look and feel. It is possible to buy most fibers in an already prepared state, worked by machines for commercial, mechanical spinners. At one time or another, you will probably want to try as many different fibers in as many states of preparation as possible. Many spinners learn one way of spinning and then spin using that method only, no matter what the circumstances. It is best not to do this, but rather to think carefully of what you are doing and to try various ways so your personal style results from thought, experience, and application, rather than from chance.

Since most contemporary spinners work on wheels with a bobbin-flyer assembly, this chapter begins with instructions for spinning on that kind of wheel and then moves into instructions for spinning on quill-type wheels. A simple form of skeining or winding spun yarn is discussed in Chapter 2, but since the spinning wheel is a fast, complex piece of equipment, there is a section in this chapter on reeling devices that are frequently used with wheels. The bobbin-flyer wheel lends itself to plying yarns and to spinning special or fancy yarns. Some of these structures and variations are discussed at the end of the chapter.

SPINNING ON THE BOBBIN-FLYER WHEEL

Before you begin to spin, lubricate the wheel so all parts run smoothly. Check the drive band by tighten-

Mellow the moonlight to shine is beginning,
Close by the window young Eileen is spinning;
Bent over the fire her blind grandmother, sitting,
Is crooning, and moaning, and drowsily knitting:—
"Eileen, anchora, I hear someone tapping."
"'Tis the ivy, dear mother, against the glass flapping."
"Eily, I surely hear somebody sighing."
"'Tis the sound, mother dear, of the summer wind dying."

    Merrily, cheerily, noiselessly whirring,
    Swings the wheel, spins the wheel, while the foot's stirring;
    Sprightly and brightly and airily ringing
    Thrills the sweet voice of the young maiden singing.

"What's that noise that I hear at the window, I wonder?"
"'Tis the little birds chirping the holly-bush under."
"What makes you be shoving and moving your stool on,
  And singing, all wrong, that old song of 'The Coolin'?"
There's a form at the casement—the form of her true love—
And he whispers, with face bent, "I'm waiting for you, love;
Get up on the stool, through the lattice step lightly,
We'll rove in the grove while the moon's shining brightly."

    Merrily, cheerily, noiselessly whirring,
    Swings the wheel, spins the wheel, while the foot's stirring;
    Sprightly and brightly and airily ringing
    Thrills the sweet voice of the young maiden singing.

The maid shakes her head, on her lips lays her fingers,
Steals up from her seat—longs to go, and yet lingers:
A frightened glance turns to her drowsy grandmother,
Puts one foot on the stool, spins the wheel with the other.
Lazily, easily, swings now the wheel round,
Slowly and lowly is heard now the reel's sound;
Noiseless and light to the lattice above her
The maid steps—then leaps to the arms of her lover.

    Slower—and slower—and slower the wheel swings;
    Lower—and lower—and lower the reel rings;
    Ere the reel and the wheel stop their ringing and moving,
    Through the grove the young lovers by moonlight are roving.

The Spinning Wheel by John Francis Waller

In the nineteenth century, women in the Cambrai district of Ireland spun on Belgium spinning wheels in cellars, where the stillness and humidity of the air assisted them in the difficult task of making yarn even finer than that produced by spinning machines.

ing and releasing the tension device. Become familiar with the wheel. Sit on a stool or sturdy chair that puts you at a comfortable height for treadling—smooth, effortless treadling is important, so begin by treadling rhythmically, not fast but steady. Some treadles require a definite and vigorous heel-toe action, while others barely need to be touched and seem to almost run by themselves. As you spin, remember that you are not seeking speed, but a slow, even action with no hesitation.

Most spinning is done by turning the wheel to the right (clockwise) to produce a Z-twist yarn. Plying or doubling is done by treadling the wheel to the left in the opposite direction. The wheel should go freely in either direction. One problem you may have as a beginner is that when you start the wheel going in one direction, it reverses, causing the yarn to unwind and tangle. Practice treadling the wheel continuously to the right and learn to stop the wheel and start it again without having it reverse. If it does not start easily on its own, give the wheel a nudge in the right direction with your hand. Once you feel confident of your ability to treadle smoothly in a clockwise direction, practice treadling the wheel continuously counterclockwise. If you stop spinning with the axle crank just over the top in the direction

you are going, it should start easily when you begin again.

Fast treadling is never necessary in spinning, and, since a slight wobble in a wheel is multiplied more and more as speed increases, overfast treadling ages and wears a wheel prematurely. Listen to the hum and whirr of your wheel, and listen too for creaks or squeaks that tell you more lubrication is needed. Minor adjustments in the connection between the treadle and the footman might be necessary for smooth treadling.

Learning to spin on a wheel requires a great deal of concentration and effort. It is important not to overlook your personal comfort while spinning. Find your favorite and most pleasing place to spin, indoors or out. Find a chair or stool that is more than just satisfactory. Try to get into a relaxed and calm state of being. Treadling barefoot tends to promote a sensitive relationship between the worker and the tool. Think of the feel and feeling of things—you should be in harmony with the tools and materials.

Once you have learned to treadle smoothly, the next step is to learn the proper adjustment of the tension devices on your particular wheel. This is best done by taking yarn already spun and running it on to the bobbin. Use a single yarn—it will twist increasingly tighter since most singles are spun to the right. Plied yarns will untwist, since they are spun to the left. (During the following exercises, treadle the wheel clockwise for a Z twist unless otherwise suggested.)

Begin with a taut tension on the drive cord. If the wheel has a single drive band controlling the flyer-spindle, then adjust the bobbin brake so it is almost taut. To begin, tie a starter thread (hairy single yarn) to the bobbin, bring it over the closest hook, reach through the orifice with your finger or with a hook (an old button hook, or something made from wire will work well), catch the thread, and draw it through. Take the already spun yarn you are going to run on to the bobbin for practice, and tie it to the end of the starter yarn. Treadle and allow the already spun yarn to spin some more and wind on to the bobbin. If the thread will not wind around the bobbin, tighten the tension. Winding on will not occur if the wheel tension devices are either too tight or too loose. Treadle slowly and regularly. Play with the tension devices until you feel a firm tug from the wheel and the thread—when lightly held—is drawn through your hands (not jerked) around the bobbin.

Try different rates of treadling, different tension adjustments, and then try applying tension with your hands. If you hold the yarn too firmly, the bobbin will slip and the thread will continue to twist,

but it will not wind until you release it. If you pull on the yarn, you can actually pull it back off the bobbin. Try stopping and then again starting the treadling. Periodically shift the yarn from hook to hook, so the bobbin fills evenly. As soon as you are comfortable when operating your wheel, you are ready to remove the practice yarn—leave the starting cord on and try spinning loose fibers into yarn.

THE SHORT DRAW

In the following descriptions of spinning the hand positions can be reversed. One spinner prefers to have the right hand nearest the wheel orifice, another the left. Being right or left-handed seems not to matter, it is more a case of which habit was developed during the learning process.

The movements for spinning on the wheel are very much like those

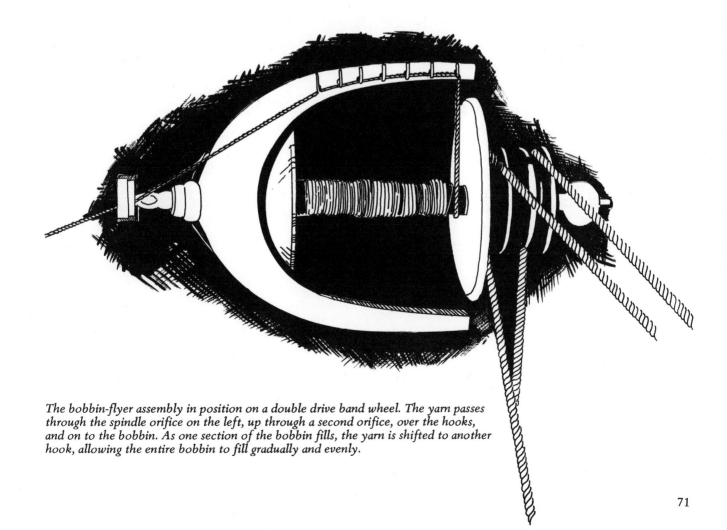

The bobbin-flyer assembly in position on a double drive band wheel. The yarn passes through the spindle orifice on the left, up through a second orifice, over the hooks, and on to the bobbin. As one section of the bobbin fills, the yarn is shifted to another hook, allowing the entire bobbin to fill gradually and evenly.

used with the drop spindle, but in wheel spinning the hands and fibers work horizontally rather than vertically, and the hands don't have to stop to turn the spindle or wind on the thread. To begin, hold the starting cord in your left hand between the thumb and fingers, about 12" out from the orifice. Overlap the starting cord with some loose fibers (tease them if necessary). Hold the starting cord and fibers firm and steady, and begin treadling. Beginners should work for a not too fine yarn, with a regular thickness and twist.

The steps for spinning are shown

are too far apart, you will have inadequate control on the tension and the fibers will not stretch out evenly. Once the fibers twist, they will no longer draft. The right hand prevents the twist from moving into the drafted fibers until they are properly attenuated. The amount of fibers drawn determines the thickness of the yarn spun.

Begin by drawing out relatively few fibers and spinning a fairly thin yarn. Thin yarns are more easily spun than thick yarns. Draw the fibers out with your right hand, and then release the pressure until you

For the short draw, the hands remain close together, some distance away from the spindle orifice. One hand holds the fiber supply and the other draws the fibers and controls the twist.

in the illustrations on page 73. The left hand controls the bulk of fibers and spreads them out between thumb and fingers in an easy rubbing motion. The right hand closes firmly over the fibers and draws them away from the left hand. The length of the draw, which is triangular-shaped (remember, the length of the draw is the widest space between left and right hands), depends on the length of the fibers.

In order to be drawn, the fibers must be able to slide past each other. If your hands are too close together, the fibers will be caught at both ends and this will prevent any sliding motion. If your hands

feel the twist—which has been building up on the other side—and let the yarn slide through. The twist will move up the drafted fibers to the greater bulk of the fibers held by your left hand. Then repeat this process, the right hand again closing over the fibers and drawing them out. If the twist moves up too far and catches undrafted fibers, your right hand may have to untwist slightly to draw the fibers properly. As your left thumb and fingers gently rub the fibers to spread them out, a base of unspun fibers is formed that prevents the twist from moving up too far.

The action of the wheel, as it pulls the yarn in, aids in drafting.

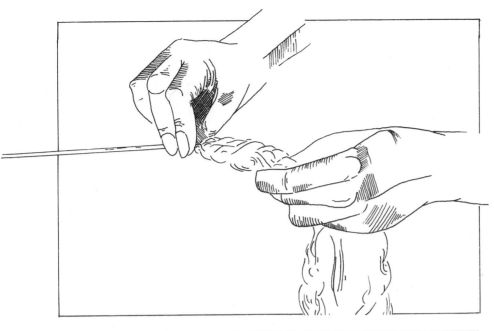

The position of the hands at the beginning of drafting. The right hand closes over the fibers, preventing the twist from moving into the loose fibers.

Draw the right hand toward the spindle orifice and away from the left to attenuate the fibers.

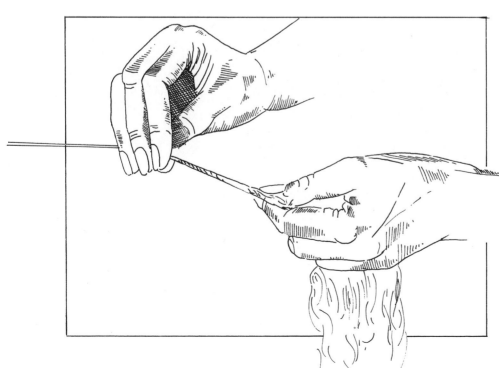

Release the pressure exerted by the right hand and allow the twist to move up into the drafted fibers.

73

Beginners frequently have problems with the yarn overtwisting—the yarn may even become so kinky that it gets caught on the hooks. This problem usually indicates that the treadling is too fast for the speed at which you are drafting. Don't treadle fast and don't clutch the yarn. Remember the old saying—"Slow feet and fast hands." Slow down on the treadling first. If the yarn continues to overtwist, tighten the tension on the drive band, specifically on the bobbin. On a single drive band with a brake on the bobbin pulley, the bobbin will not wind if the tension is either too tight or too loose.

As the bobbin fills, shift the yarn from one hook to another. Some flyers have hooks on both arms that are slightly offset so once the yarn has been shifted along one arm it can then be shifted back along the second set of hooks to fill in depressions. As the bobbin

The short draw method of spinning with the hand motions reversed. The fiber supply is held in the right hand and the fibers are drafted with the left. The wheel actually draws the fibers from the lightly held rolag (sausage-shaped bunch of fibers).

fills, its diameter changes, and this affects the twist. Minor adjustment to increase the winding-on rate, in order to maintain twist uniformly, can be made as the bobbin fills. This is done because as the bobbin diameter increases, the yarn is not wound on quite as quickly. Slightly increasing tension on the bobbin as it fills will compensate for the larger diameter.

As soon as you become comfortable with the spinning method just described, try reversing your hand motions and draw to the left as illustrated on pages 74 and 75. During spinning, the hands can be very flexible, moving back and forth, manicuring the yarn, and coaxing in loose fibers. As soon as you become confident, and the spinning is relatively effortless, try what is called the long draw. This method is similar to spinning on the heavy supported spindle where the drafting is done between the

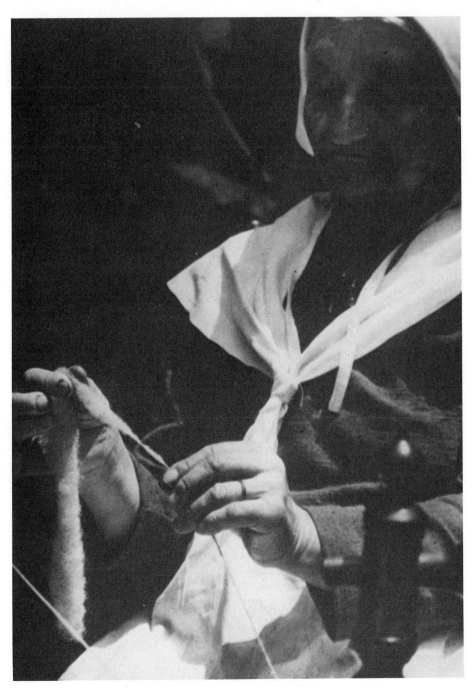

Spinning a fine thread from wool fibers prepared for spinning by carding them into a rolag. The right hand draws the fibers and allows the twist to move up. Thin places in the fibers take the twist first.

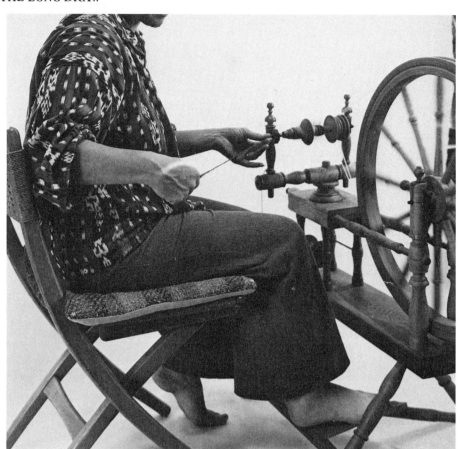

For the long draw, keep the left hand close to the orifice, regulating the twist. Draw the right hand back, stretching and drafting the fibers just ahead of the moving twist.

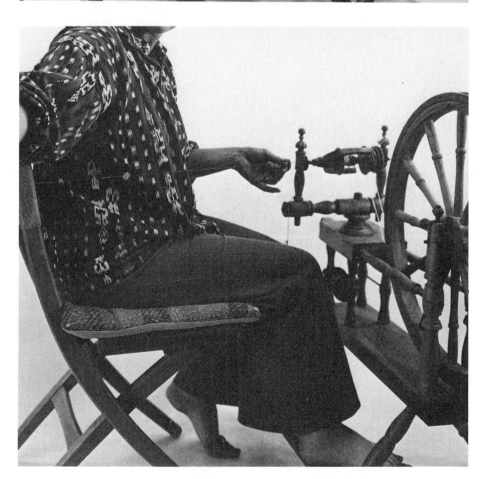

Sweep the right hand back as far as the arm will stretch, then release the left hand, and quickly wind the spun yarn on to the bobbin.

twist and one hand rather than between the two hands.

THE LONG DRAW

Begin spinning with your hands just a few inches apart. Keep the left hand closed on the spun yarn close to the orifice, and hold the loose fibers lightly in your right hand. There should not yet be any twist between your hands. Hold steady for a moment, and allow the twist to build up in the short space between the spindle orifice and the left hand. At this point, release the grip on the twist held by your left fingers, and at the same time draw back with the right hand. The left hand should stay close to the orifice and should gently regulate the twist by opening and closing on the yarn. There should be a definite pull on the growing yarn, or the twist will not run up. Some of the pull comes from the wheel, and some from the opening and closing motion of the left hand. The pull from the right hand as it draws farther and farther back should be strong enough to prevent the yarn from winding on to the bobbin until the right arm is fully outstretched.

Remember that thin areas in the yarn will take the twist before the thicker sections will. Notice too that once the fibers are twisted they won't draw, and that, as the right hand draws back, the twist runs up and catches the thin spots first and leaves the thick places unspun. Further stretching by drawing back on the right hand attenuates the thick places.

Once the right arm is stretched out and the yarn is properly spun, release the left hand and move the right hand quickly toward the orifice without allowing the yarn to slacken. Stop close to the orifice, allowing enough room to repeat the cycle. The treadling and the hand motions should be smooth

and rhythmical. Be flexible with your spinning. There is no right or wrong way. Speed and rhythm come with practice—don't be discouraged if your first efforts fail. With thought and practice, spinning will become easy and enjoyable.

SPINNING ON QUILL WHEELS

On a quill wheel, spinning is done off the tip of the spindle or quill. The spinner must hold the growing thread in such a way that the rotating spindle imparts twist. Once a length of yarn is spun, the yarn is guided on to the spindle shaft. Spinning and winding alternate, and the process is slower than on the bobbin-flyer assembly, which permits simultaneous spinning and winding. The process for spinning on handpowered quill wheels necessarily requires the long draw, because one hand must turn the wheel as the other draws out the

On this electric wheel, the speed is controlled by pressing on a foot peddle. The spinner is pulling off bits of unspun fibers before allowing yarn to wind on to the bobbin.

Traditionally, a corn husk rather then a starting cord is used on the spindle of the walking wheel. The corn husk is bound in two places with fine thread to hold the husk, which is left on the spindle after the yarn is removed. To begin, take a rolag of carded fleece and allow a few loose fibers to wind on to the husk by turning the wheel clockwise.

As the first fibers wind, shift the hand holding the fibers to the left so the loose fibers are brought to the tip, where spinning occurs. Draw back your left hand, allowing a few fibers to stretch out and twist. Turn the wheel slightly to run enough twist up to spin the loose fibers, and then shift the left hand to the right and turn the wheel slightly counterclockwise so the thread unwinds from the spindle tip to the point of attachment. Turn the wheel clockwise to wind this first short length around the corn husk to get a solid beginning to work from.

fibers. The addition of a treadle leaves both hands free to manipulate the fibers, but spinning remains intermittent, since each arm's length of yarn must still be guided on to the spindle shaft.

SPINNING ON THE WALKING WHEEL

The walking wheel is a popular form of the quill-type wheel. The great circumference of the drive wheel requires that the person spinning step from drive wheel to quill with each spinning-winding cycle. The walking wheel shown in the step-by-step illustrations on pages 80 to 82 was designed and built by C. Norman Hicks. In the photographs, he demonstrates the method he uses for spinning on his many walking wheels. This version, named "Eunice" (from unicycle), is made from a bicycle wheel, a radio, fan parts, and plywood. Mr. Hicks spins with washed wool carded into rolags.

To spin on the walking wheel, the right hand turns the wheel clockwise, and spinning occurs off the spindle tip as the left hand stretches out a short section of a rolag first into a loose roving, which becomes twisted into yarn at its thinnest spots. Further pulling and turning stretches the remaining roving sections until they too become yarn. It is a self-equalizing process that tends to eliminate thick and thin areas. Then the wheel is stopped, reversed to unwind the yarn from the tip, and again turned clockwise to wind the yarn on to the spindle shaft near the whorl, leaving just enough exposed yarn to again wind off the tip in order to continue the cycle.

The traditional way of starting is to use a corn husk, but many spinners just tie a starting cord around the spindle shaft. To begin, attach a starting cord or take a dry corn husk (wet it until you start), and wrap it around the spindle, leaving the spindle tip exposed. Tie both ends with fine thread to hold the husk in place. The corn husk acts almost like a magnet to the wool, and the loose fibers hold to it as the first spin is put in. Catch a few loose fibers in the crack formed where the corn husk overlaps itself. Turn the wheel slowly, so, as the spindle turns, the loose fibers stick to the husk. At the same time, shift the left hand to the spindle tip so, as the hand draws back—attentuating fibers—the twist runs up the loose, stretched fibers to the hand. Do this for just a short length, slowly and carefully in order to get a good beginning. Now turn the wheel counterclockwise a slight bit, and unwind the fibers from the tip; then turn clockwise again, and wind this short beginning length on to the corn husk to anchor the beginning. Now proceed, spinning as shown in the illustrations.

Always leave just enough of the spun length to bring the yarn out to the spindle tip and start the next draw (see Step 1). Draw the left hand back, allowing part of the rolag of loose fibers to slip through the fingers of your left hand, grasp firmly once again with the left hand, and draw quickly back, as shown in Step 2. The twist in the previously spun yarn that has not been wound will run up to keep the fibers from collapsing, but not enough to stop them from drawing. Shift the hand to move the yarn out on the spindle tip and turn the wheel to impart more twist (Step 3). The thin areas will twist first, and, as the hand and body move further back, the thick areas will draw and twist. If you want a very smooth yarn, hold the length taut and pull off bits and pieces of fiber with your right hand (Step 4). Then, while maintaining tension on the yarn, shift it close to

Step 1. As the first length is wound on to the spindle shaft, spiral the last 5 or 6" toward the tip of the spindle so no more than 1" of the already spun yarn extends beyond the tip to begin the next full draw.

Step 2. Shift the left hand about 4" farther back on the rolag, grasp the fibers tightly, and draw back with the left hand. The twist from the length of previously spun yarn will shift upward into the unspun fibers—this light twist is usually just enough to hold the drafted fibers together.

Step 3. Just as the left hand completes the operation described, shift the hand leftward until the partially spun fibers between left hand and the tip of the spindle make an angle of about 30° with the bed of the great wheel. As you turn the wheel clockwise with the right hand, the yarn should "fall off" the tip each time the spindle rotates, twisting the yarn being spun. At the correct angle, the yarn neither rolls on to the spindle, nor does it tend to unwind. With practice comes the coordination of turning and pulling, producing even-sized yarn. When the diameter is satisfactory, stop pulling with the left hand, but continue to turn with the right hand until the desired degree of twist is achieved.

Step 4. If a smooth yarn is desired, hold the just-formed yarn taut and pull off bits and pieces of fuzz.

Step 5. Shift the left hand closer to the wheel to bring the just-spun yarn parallel to the bed of the wheel. Usually the left hand will describe a wide arc over and perhaps behind the head in order to keep the yarn taut as you turn the wheel counterclockwise with the right hand just enough to unwind the yarn from the tip. Then turn the wheel clockwise to wind the yarn on to the spindle. Follow the yarn down to the spindle with the left hand, maintaining enough tension to keep the yarn taut. Leave just enough spun yarn unwound to allow a beginning for the next cycle.

the wheel (Step 5). At the same time, reverse the wheel to unwind the yarn from the tip, and then wind it on to the shaft by turning the wheel clockwise. As spinning continues, build up a nice, even cone shape on the spindle.

As you go through these motions and they become rhythmical, you will find that you are continually stepping forward and backward.

There is a slight variation on the method of spinning described that is frequently used by spinners especially when spinning short fibers. Instead of grasping the loose fibers firmly and pulling back so the fibers draw with just a little twist (which keeps the arrangement from collapsing before final twisting and further attenuation), the spinner draws back the left hand, allowing the right amount of fibers to slip through the fingers just as the twist moves up and catches them. If the

yarn consistently overspins, you are turning the wheel too much. If the wheel is turning but no twist is moving up the fibers, you are probably not holding the yarn off the tip in the right position—when just the right position is found, there is a vibration from the tip as the twist moves up. While drawing the fibers, too much pull will cause the drive band to slip on the spindle pulley and consequently no spinning will happen. If the fibers will not slip, they already have been twisted too much. Drop the rolag at the end of the half-spun yarn, and let it unwind by itself several turns. Then pick up the rolag and try to slip the fibers again. You may have to repeat this untwisting to get it to the correct condition. If the fibers are underspun, give an extra turn to the wheel and run more twist up before shifting the hand to wind the yarn on.

Spinning on a walking wheel. This wheel from the early nineteenth century has a Minor's accelerating head, which greatly increases the speed on the spindle.

Spinning on an East Asian type wheel is very much like spinning on the walking wheel, but here the spinner sits. Spinning is still done off the tip, and the wheel is reversed to put the thread in the correct position for winding. Since the spinner is seated, the draw of the left hand cannot extend beyond the reach of the arm. This small charka with horizontally fitted drive wheels is designed to spin fine cotton thread. The wheel case can be clamped to a table or held steady on the floor with a knee or foot.

SPINNING ON THE EAST ASIAN QUILL WHEEL

Spinning on the East Asian quill wheel involves the same hand motions and principles as spinning on the walking wheel, but such spinning does not call for the total body movement. The spinner squats or sits; the arm is first drawn back as far as possible, and then moved back toward the spindle as the yarn is wound on. Westerners usually are not accustomed to sitting on the floor level and frequently prefer to clamp this kind of wheel to a table so they can stand or sit in a chair while working.

SPINNING ON THE QUILL WHEEL WITH TREADLE

Spinning on the quill wheel that is equipped with a treadle is much faster than working on the hand-powered wheel. The process is somewhat different because both hands are free to manipulate the fibers. Treadling is continuous, and the wheel turns in one direction without the stopping and reversing characteristic of hand-driven wheels. Fibers are still spun off the spindle tip, but the orientation of the body is totally different. Alden Amos demonstrates his style in the nearby photographs on a wheel he designed and built. Treadling is continuous as fibers are drawn out to arms length and then guided with the left hand to wind on to the quill. The main problem is building the yarn up gradually on the quill with even tension. The head on the wheel shown can be turned and angled to facilitate spinning and to provide greater comfort. Problems in quill-type treadle spinning primarily concern tension or yarn preparation. Practice is the key—once you intellectually understand, you have to work through feel.

Spinning on a quill wheel with a treadle is different from spinning on either the walking wheel or the East Asian wheel. The spinner sits, treadling the wheel continuously in one direction. Spinning still occurs off the tip, but both hands are free to manipulate the fibers. This photograph shows the beginning of the draw. The left hand holds the fiber supply and moves quickly back as the twist runs up, nipping at the unspun fibers. The right hand acts as a guide and twist regulator.

The left hand extends way back to full arm's length.

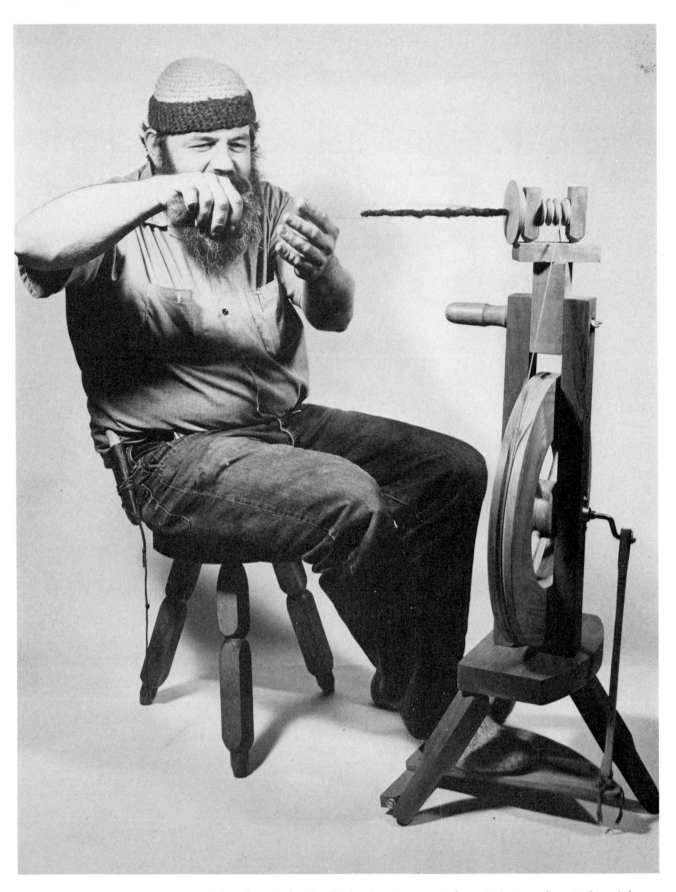

Then the right hand pulls the thread over so it first winds on to the spindle and then guides it back so it again spins off the tip to continue the cycle.

REMOVING THE SPUN YARN

Once the fibers are spun into yarn and the quill or bobbin is full, the yarn must be removed. With the hand spindle or quill wheel, the wound cone of yarn can be slipped off the spindle intact, or, as with bobbins, the yarn can be wound into balls or reeled into skeins. For setting the twist, washing, or dyeing, the yarn must be formed into skeins. Simple methods for winding skeins as well as for setting the twist are discussed in Chapter 2, but special kinds of reels are often used with spinning wheels.

A reel is faster and more efficient than either the niddy-noddy or the simpler hand-to-elbow technique. A reel is basically a pronged device that rotates on a central axis, somewhat like a windmill, The yarn is wound around the edge of the projecting arms to form a skein, the size of which is determined by the diameter of the outside of the reel. It is usually a set measurement, so yardage can be easily calculated.

A reeler can be very simply notched sticks or bamboo tied together with the center axis stuck into a bottle or hole for easy turning. A plain, very sturdy reel is shown on page 88, along with a more complex reel with turned elements and a counting device.

Yarn can be reeled directly from the bobbin, or the bobbin can be removed. To reel spun yarn with the bobbin still in position on the wheel, shift the drive band or brake off the bobbin pulley so the bobbin turns freely on the spindle. Then pull the yarn free of the spindle orifice and flyer hooks. Take the yarn directly from the bobbin to the reel in such a way that it does not catch on the flyer hooks. Turn the reel with one hand (sometimes there is a handle), and guide the yarn with the other hand. The bobbin can also be removed from the wheel and held on a dowel for reeling. With a quill type wheel, the drive band is simply slipped off the spindle pulley before winding.

The yarn must be formed into skeins for setting the twist, for washing, or for dyeing, but if the yarn is to be plied or used as spun it can be wound off into a ball. A contemporary ball winder widely used by hand spinners is shown on page 88. It is hand operated, and very quickly forms the yarn into a squarish ball that has an open center. These balls are firmly wound, but not so tight as to unduly stretch the yarn. The balls are perfect for plying two yarns, because the end in the center can be matched with the outer end—there is no waste and no problem with tangled yarn.

When skeins of yarn are ready to be used or unwound, they are placed on a swift. Swifts are always adjustable to accommodate varying size skeins. One such swift, an umbrella swift that is widely used for this purpose, is on page 89.

PLYING

Plying refers to the process of spinning two or more already spun yarns together. It is easy to do, and beginners frequently ply commercially spun yarns to gain familiarity with the spindle and spinning wheel. Yarns are plied for strength, for bulk, and for combining different colors and kinds or textures of yarns. Many weavers and knitters prefer plied yarns because they have less tendency to pill or break. Plying is usually done on a bobbin-flyer spinning wheel, because winding is even and continuous and both hands are free to manipulate and tension the threads.

How to spin the most generally useful plied yarn—and the one most

An antique table top clock reel. The number of revolutions the wheel turns is counted and indicated on the clocklike face. On the base at the lower left is a series of slots that allow the reeler to adjust the position of the yarn as it winds. In this way, the skein is made up of a number of neat little sections—the skein can be tied off to maintain this order. The crosspiece on the end of the arm with the handle may be shifted to ease the removal of the skein.

(Above) A simple standing reel with a sturdy base. The spinner places a foot on the base to stabilize the reel while winding the spun yarn into a skein. The arm on the bottom left has a pin arranged so the U-shaped end-piece can be easily removed.

(Left) Ball winders work very quickly and efficiently. Many spinners use them for winding yarn off spindles and wheel when no washing or dyeing is to be done. Such wound balls work very nicely for plying two yarns. When yarn is to be plied, it may be started on the wheel by beginning with the yarn end from the inside of the ball and also with the yarn end from the outside of the ball. This technique eliminates the problem of unequal lengths and multiple balls.

(Above) When skeins of yarn are ready to be used, they are traditionally placed on a swift that prevents them from tangling during unwinding. Swifts are adjustable to accommodate many sizes of skeins. This horizontally mounted umbrella swift is often mounted vertically, but many spinners strongly favor the horizontal position. When it is used in the vertical position, parts of uneven or tangled skeins can droop and get caught in the apparatus. This swift spreads outward and inward much as an umbrella does. A large wooden screw clamps it to a support, and a smaller screw holds the ribs in position. When the swift is not in use, the screw is released and the ribs gather in toward the center.

This is one method of plying two threads on the bobbin-flyer wheel. One hand acts as a guide and regulates the twist. The other hand holds the threads—one between the thumb and index finger, the other between the index and middle fingers. The hand positions may be reversed, depending on your preference.

often produced—is described below.

Step 1. Using the spinning wheel, spin two bobbins or two balls of yarn with a good overtwist. Spin the threads in the normal manner by treadling, so the wheel turns in a clockwise direction. Many spinning wheels come with extra bobbins and some come with built-in bobbin racks or detached racks, called lazy kates, which hold the extra bobbins during plying or when they are not in use.

Step 2. Place the balls in individual small baskets or boxes and the bobbins on a spool rack. A simple rack can be made using sturdy wire (coat hanger wire) and a box (shoebox). Perforate the box sides with the wire ends in such a way that the bobbins can be suspended on the wire. The bobbins should turn freely as yarn is drawn from them. Plying can also be done from a single ball wound in such a way as to leave both ends exposed.

Step 3. Before beginning to ply, tighten the tension devices on the wheel for a good strong bobbin pull. Tie the two threads previously spun to the starting cord, and pass the threads over the right hand by running one thread between the thumb and index finger and down across the palm. Pass the other thread over the same index finger near the tip, then loop it back between the index and middle fingers.

Step 4. Treadle the wheel so it turns counterclockwise to produce an S-twist yarn. As the yarns are drawn through the fingers and spun together, the overtwist of the individual yarns will be taken out and the two yarns will naturally twist together. The left hand should rest near the orifice, acting as a guide and controlling the twist.

Plying in General. The hand positions can be reversed, depending on what is most comfortable for you. The threads should be kept separated for an even flow and proper tension control, but what is illustrated is only one method of holding the threads, and many variations are possible. The illustration on page 91 shows one way of holding three strands to make a three-ply yarn. Two or more overspun Z-twist yarns (clockwise) when plied S twist (counterclockwise) will produce a yarn in which the fibers naturally intertwine and hold together. The overtwist on the single yarns untwists during plying and the yarn produced is soft, even, and strong. The surface texture on two yarns spun together with the twisting sequence described above is different from the surface structure that results from spinning three yarns together. The visual difference is shown in the illustration on page 92.

The bobbin-flyer spinning wheel is an excellent tool for plying. Both hands are free to control how the yarns are fed in, and treadling produces a steady pull, which draws the yarns firmly and evenly from the hands. Plying can also be done on the spindle and on quill wheels, but the process is slower and it is more difficult to control the twist. Plying on the hand spindle and a complete description of S twist and Z twist is given in Chapter 2. When plying on quill wheels that are turned by hand, the drive band can be crossed between the drive wheel and spindle pulley. This reverses the spin, but allows the spinner to still turn the wheel clockwise.

Many different yarns can be produced depending on various twist combinations and variations in how the individual threads are fed into the orifice. Plied yarns can

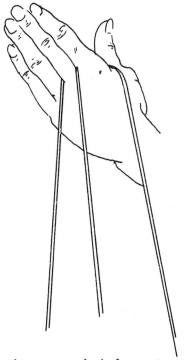

This is one method of separating and holding three strands for spinning a three-ply yarn.

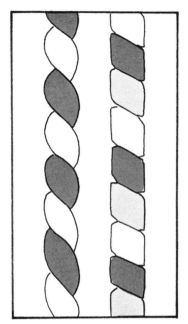

Two and three-ply yarns have different surface textures as a result of the way the Z-twist yarns naturally hold together in the S-twist ply.

On quill wheels, the drive band is sometimes twisted so it crosses between the spindle pulley and the drive wheel. This crossing over or "closing of the band" is often done for plying. It allows the spinner to turn the wheel in the more comfortable clockwise direction while producing a counterclockwise rotation of the spindle.

be plied with other plied yarns. One thread can be held tight, and the other loosely—the tight thread becomes a central core, and the other wraps around it. Many yarn structures can be easily produced by combining different kinds of yarn, such as a thick and a thin yarn or a tightly twisted smooth yarn with a loosely twisted fuzzy yarn. Other kinds and lengths of fibers can be allowed to grab in as the yarns twist together. Many variations are possible and unique, special yarns can be created. Unique yarns, sometimes referred to as novelty yarns, can be produced by plying yarns under different tension by controlling one yarn with each hand, a method some spinners prefer even for normal plying. The yarns being plied are usually held between thumb and index fingers. If the tips of the forefingers just barely touch, an even flow at the same consistent angle can be easily maintained.

YARN STRUCTURE AND DESIGN

Once you become an experienced wheel spinner and feel comfortable with your wheel, you can start developing even greater control. How fibers are prepared, whether fed into the wheel as tangled masses or straightened into a parallel smooth arrangement, mixed or blended, all fine, all coarse, or a random mixture, determines what kind of yarn is spun. Methods of fiber preparation and individual fiber characteristics are discussed in the following chapters. They will give you insight into a great variety of possible yarns. How you as the spinner allow the fibers to feed into the twist during spinning and plying also has a great deal to do with the final texture and design of the yarn. Some of the possibilities are shown in the illustration. Knowledge of how a yarn is formed assures a better understanding of how the yarn will respond when used for constructing textiles.

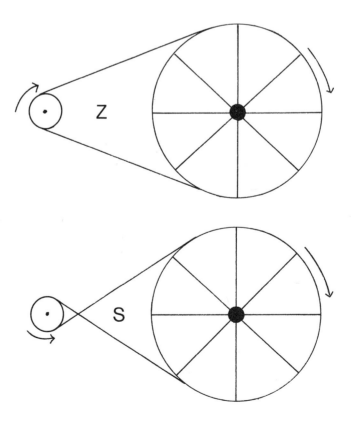

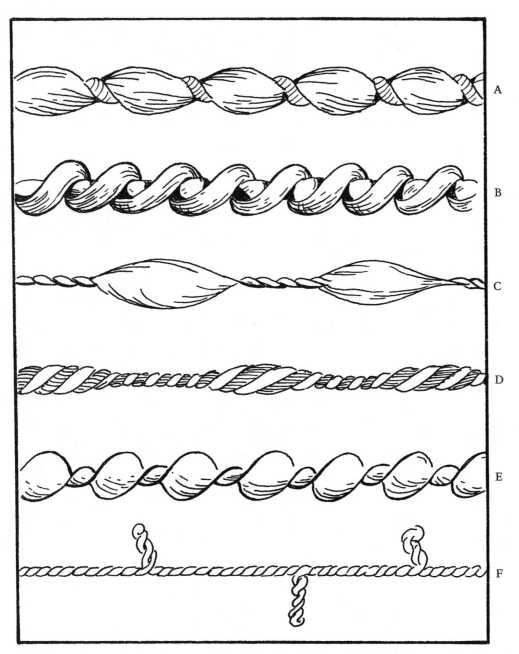

Six of many variations possible in yarn structure. (A) A thick, soft, S-twist short-fibered yarn, and a thin, smooth, long-fibered yarn with a Z twist. The two yarns are plied with a Z twist. (B) A soft yarn spun with a Z twist and a firm, thin yarn spun with an S twist. The two are plied with an S twist, which accentuates the twist on the thin yarn. To make this yarn, put tension on the thin yarn during plying, and allow the thicker yarn to pass quickly. (C) This is a single yarn with thick, unspun areas called slubs. The slubs are created as part of the yarn design. To make this yarn, use the short draw. At appropriate intervals, grasp a large amount of unspun fibers between the thumb and index finger of the drafting hand. Don't allow the grasped fibers to draw out. This will form a thick unspun area, or slub. The thin drawn-out areas will take all the twist. These slubs can be created at either regular or irregular intervals. (D) This yarn is a combination of two unevenly plied different colored yarns. To construct such a yarn, spin two strands of differing colors in one direction, and then ply them in the opposite direction. During plying, pull back on the yarns in some places to allow extra twist to run up. In other places hurry the yarns toward the orifice, and permit as little twist as possible. (E) This example is composed of two yarns, one thick and one fine, spun in the same direction and then plied in the opposite direction. (F) To make this yarn, spin one overtwisted yarn and another slightly thicker yarn with a normal amount of twist. Both of these yarns should be spun in the same direction. Ply in the opposite direction. During plying, hold back on the thicker yarn and periodically rush the overtwisted yarn toward the orifice. This forward motion creates an excess, which results in curled nubs.

CHAPTER FIVE

Building a Spinning Wheel

Show me a sight,
   Bates for delight,
   An ould Irish wheel wid a young Irish girl at it.
O! no!
Nothin' you'll show
   Aquals her sittin' and talkin' a twirl at it.
Look at her there,
Night in her hair—
The blue ray of day from her eye
      Laughin' out on us!
   Faix an a foot
   Perfect of cut,
Peepin' to put an end to all
                  Doubt in us.

See! the lambs' wool
Turns coarse an' Dull
By them soft, beautiful,
      Weeshy, white hands of her.
   Down goes her heel,
   Round runs the wheel,
Purrin wid pleasure to take
            The commands of her.

A.P. Graves

A sturdy bench wheel, with a large orifice and bobbin—such a wheel can be built easily by the home carpenter. The wheel spins a range of yarns from fine to bulky and is inexpensive to build.

John Gieling, a San Francisco designer, and I set out to design and build a quality spinning wheel that could be built by the home carpenter who had little woodworking experience and no fancy tools. We wanted to find commonly available parts, so anyone building the wheel according to our design would find the task quick and simple. We also wanted the wheel to be sturdy, completely functional, esthetically pleasing, and cheap. Quill wheels, along the line of the traditional walking wheel, can be made with even less difficulty, but spinning is slow on them and most modern handspinners want something faster—any spinner with an eye toward production and comfort wants a wheel with a treadle and flyer. This requirement calls for a sophisticated apparatus with a number of moving parts.

Although wheels can be built without using power tools, such tools make the task much, much easier. We found that a table saw or radial arm saw and a drill press were essential in order to maintain high quality and precise workmanship. A band saw is best for the curved cuts, but we found that a saber saw, when handled carefully, could do the job. Many pieces are notched so they interlock and support properly. Drilling straight holes is very important to keep parts aligned and to avoid wheel or pulley wobble.

We wanted to build a spinner that was not just minimally acceptable, but that performed in a manner equivalent to something you might expect to buy in a shop. We also wanted a versatile wheel that would spin either a thin or a heavy yarn and that would be comfortable and smooth.

The instructions in this chapter are meant not only to show you how to make an excellent spinning wheel step-by-step, but also to present an idea to the more general reader of the kinds of problems one might encounter when building a wheel. My experience in buying wheels is that cheap models come in fir and plywood, and the expensive models come in hardwood. If you have the money and are particularly concerned about a beautiful appearance, you would probably be better off buying the expensive model. In making your own wheel, all sorts of possibilities are open. Scrap wood that you or a friend might have, or some particular local wood that is special to you, can be used to make the wheel less expensive and more personal.

Certain parts of a spinning wheel are complex or tricky. If you are an experienced woodworker and have access to a wood lathe, your solution to a particular problem might be different and perhaps better than ours. A change in one part will lead to other changes, so be sure to think through the entire process. This is why a concise list of materials used is placed at the end rather than at the beginning of this chapter. Before you begin construction, study the wheels shown in various parts of this book, and, if possible, spin on different wheels. Read this chapter completely, and then carefully follow our instructions or use your imagination plus what you have available to build your own spinning wheel.

FIRST DECISIONS

Before construction starts, certain key decisions must be made. The large drive wheel determines, to a certain extent, the size of the frame. If you decide to use some other kind of wheel, or if you decide to make or use a wheel of a different diameter, you might need to change the mounting device

This is a front view of the totally assembled spinning wheel. The drive wheel is made from particle board and the bobbin shaft from the hollow end of a window shade core.

This is a back view of the spinning wheel—the wheel axle is assembled from standard plumbing parts.

MATERIALS FOR BUILDING A WHEEL

Wood

Hardwood (maple): 7" x 9" x 1"

Softwood (redwood): 113" of 2x2
144" of 2x1
15" of 1x6
50" of 1x2
26" of 1x1

Plywood (5/8" exterior): 13" x 7"

Particle Board (3/4"): 16" x 33"

Hardware

Flathead wood screws: 30 of 2x12
8 of 3/4x12
7 of 1-1/4x8
4 of 1-1/2x8
2 of 1x8

Brass screws: 1 of 3/4"

Screw eye: 1 small

Bolts: 2 of 2-1/2" with 4 wing nuts and 5 washers
1 of 1/4" roundhead
1 of 2-1/2" hexhead with washer

Floor flanges: 2 for 1/2" pipe

Pipe: 1 piece 1/2" with 2" nipple
1 piece 1/2" with 2-1/2" nipple

Cap for 1/2" pipe

Shank washer (B-15)

Hose washers: 5 with 3/4" inner diameter

O rings: 1-3/4"
1-7/8"

Aluminum tubing: 3/4" outside diameter

Cup hooks: 6 with 1/2" opening

Iron rod: 15" long, 3/8" thick

MISCELLANEOUS

Wooden tubing: 16" of 7/8" diameter hollow wood
(window shade tubing) 1/2" long hollow
tube 6/8" diameter

Drive band for a treadle sewing machine, 65" long

Rubber band

Seine twine

and frame arrangement. The most difficult part to come up with, and something you should not begin without, is the hollow shaft of the bobbin that slides over the tube of the flyer. A second section of this same shaft acts as a spacer between the bobbin and the back maiden. On our wheel, the first piece measures 14" and the second 2". Making this hollow tube, even with a wood lathe, is no simple task. Our solution was to use the core of a large window shade blind—part of every window blind core is hollow.

Once you find a tube to use for the bobbin shaft and spacer, locate another tube that will fit easily inside it. This second tube will become the spindle shaft and must be hollow, at least at one end. Our solution was to use aluminum tube-conduit. As the yarn spins, it goes into the end of the metal spindle tube and up through another hole to the hooks on to the flyer. The size of the yarn you spin cannot be larger than the inside diameter of the spindle tube. The bobbin shaft and spacer could be made of a sturdy cardboard or plastic tube. It is also possible to make the inner part wood, and the outer part metal.

CONSTRUCTING THE SPINNING WHEEL

The entire spinning wheel can be made of hardwood, but hardwood is expensive and often more difficult to work with. There are five small parts that take a lot of wear, and these should definitely be made of hardwood. We used 1" thick maple.

The Frame. The first step in making the spinning wheel is to construct the frame. The fourteen different parts, with measurements included, are shown in the first illustration, and the pieces are shown assembled

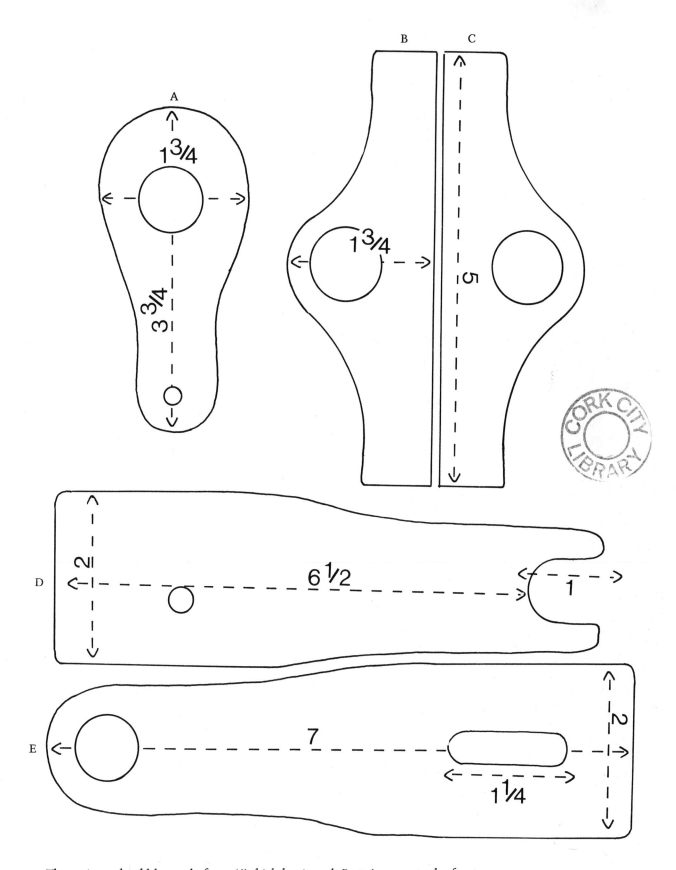

CORK CITY LIBRARY

These pieces should be made from 1" thick hardwood. Part A connects the front axle to the treadle footman. Parts B and C are mounts that hold the wheel axles. Parts D and E are the supports, or maidens, that carry the flyer assembly. Don't cut the inner holes until necessary, since the size may vary depending on the parts they carry.

The structural pieces that form the frame, numbered from top to bottom in sequential order of assembly. Redwood is used in this example, but a stronger wood such as fir would offer more support. Parts 1, 2, 3, and 4 are the four corner posts, each a 28" long 2 x 2. Parts 5, 6, 7, and 8 are 24" long 1 x 2's. Part 9, which is just barely visible, is a solid iron curtain rod 15" long and ⅜" in diameter. Parts 12 and 13 are each 16½" long 1 x 2's and 14 is a 13⅛" long 1 x 2.

The structural supports are notched for a proper fit by drawing the saw blade back and forth. A dado blade or chisel might also be used.

The basic frame assembled.

in the second. Wood measurements vary in different kinds and grades of wood. A 1 x 2 never actually measures that, so expect variations and discrepancies. Any wood you use should be dry. We used redwood, which for us is a local softwood with a beautiful look and feel. If you are a large person, or like the feel of an especially roomy wheel, you might want to make the structure wider or higher. Any sturdy rod can be used for item 9. Part 14 acts as a spacer and fits between the two front uprights under the rod. It is the last part of the frame to go together, and should fit snugly—so wait until you are ready for it before making the final cut. For assembly, you will need thirty No. 12 flathead wood screws each 2" long. We recommend thick screws for softwoods, such as redwood; thinner screws for fir; and even thinner ones for hardwood. Countersink all screws. Notch the frame pieces for structural support, and drill guide holes for the screws with a drill press.

You should sand the edges and any rough spots both before and after assembling the pieces. Be careful not to cinch the screws down too tightly in the softwood, or the threads formed in the wood will strip. The frame should end up being true to square. Use a square to make sure the cuts are correct and keep an eye on things as the pieces go together. Do not glue anything until the entire spinning wheel is together, and then only glue pieces that for one reason or another should fit tightly but do not.

A study of the illustrations on pages 100 and 101 will show you how the notching system works. Put the frame together in numerical sequence beginning with No. 1. The notches on 1, 2, 3, and 4 begin 15½" down from the top. They end up being on the outside and accommodate 5 and 6. The sanded depressions on these pieces are made to allow room for the drive wheel and do not have to be done until later. Parts 7 and 8 go on the inside bottom on the sides—they are notched to fit against 1 and 4 and 2 and 3. They should clear the floor by 1". Drill a hole on the inside of 1 and 2 ½" above 7 and 8, for the rod (9) to slide into. Parts 10 and 11 also span the frame and are notched to fit on top of 5 and 6. The placement of 11 might vary if a different kind of wheel is used. On this model, the space between 10 and 11 is 3¼". Parts 12 and 13 are the top cross members. They are notched at the ends to accommodate the corner posts, and go on the inside of the frame. They are also notched in the center (2" wide, ¼" deep) to receive the maidens. Part 14 rests 1" behind the rod, level with 7 and 8—it is secured with one screw on each side. The frame should be square and level.

The Wheel. We chose to use ¾" particle board doubled for the wheel. Plywood could be used, but it presents more problems. The wheel needs to be heavy for momentum and in balance with the large bobbin and flyer. A heavy wheel tends to anchor the entire structure. Any number of ready-made wheels could be used in place of the one we suggest here. This wheel has a 16" diameter. To make it using ¾" particle board, describe two circles, each with an 8" radius. Eventually, parts of the wheel will be drilled out to make the rim heavier, creating better momentum. These cut-outs should be balanced so the wheel is not thrown off—any balanced method of drilling holes of any size can be used. The design we used is shown on the next page.

This is a diagram used to arrange the cut-outs for the wheel. The actual wheel has a 16" diameter, with 2½" holes and ¼" holes. A 3" metal flange will later be attached to the center with 4 screws, as indicated in the diagram. It is important that the cut-outs not interfere.

A pilot hole should be drilled in the center of each piece of particle board. Such a hole will act as a guide when the particle board is later cut into a a disc (especially when cutting with a band saw).

Spread white glue over the inside of each wheel.

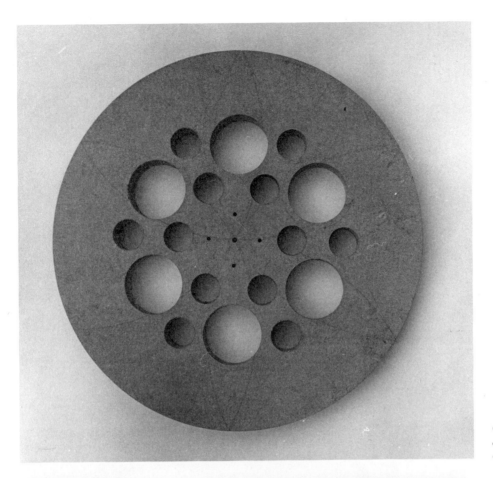

Clamp the two sections together and allow them to dry before drilling.

Drill the wheel using an adjustable-hole saw. The large holes are 2½" in diameter and the small 1¼". Any well-balanced design would be appropriate.

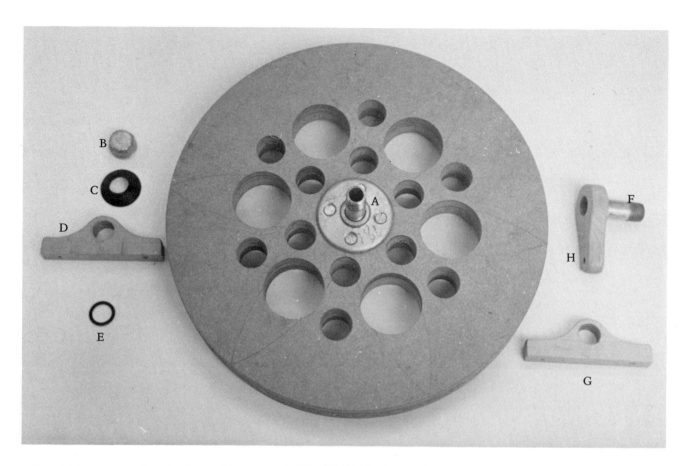

(Above) The parts for the wheel assembly are shown here in sequential order beginning at the back of the wheel: part A is a 2" nipple (½" pipe); B is a ½" pipe cap; C is a shank washer; and D is a hardwood piece cut out earlier. Part A goes through D and is screwed down to the frame. Part E is a ¾" O ring, and F is a 2½" nipple (½" pipe) that screws into the flange on the other side. The other end of the nipple is screwed into a hardwood piece cut out earlier. Part F goes through G, which mounts to the frame.

The back of the wheel assembled.

A front view of the wheel assembled.

It is very important that the wheel be perfectly round, and that the center be clearly marked. Although there will be an axle on each side and nothing that goes through the wheel, drill a hole through the center of each round section to act as a guide (see illustration on page 104). Insert a bolt or nail that is anchored to another board, which in turn can be clamped to the band saw table. Rotate the wheel on its axis, allowing the band saw to cut it perfectly round. Turn it round and round slowly so the blade does not bend. After cutting the wheel, tip the band saw plate so you can saw off at an angle about 1/16" on the inside of each wheel section. When the two sections are glued and clamped, a slight depression will be formed in the center for the drive band to track on. You can also form the depression with a rasp, either before or after the wheel is assembled.

After the glue dries, drill the cut-outs. Center floor flanges for ½" pipe on each side of the wheel, and mount them with No. 12 flathead screws ¾" long (8). Flanges are common plumbing fittings and can be found at any hardware store. It is very important that they be exactly in the center. The holes drilled in the wheel should not be so close to the center that they interfere with the flanges. The guide holes for the flange screws as well as the diagram for the pattern we used are shown in the illustration on page 105.

All the wheel assembly parts are shown in the illustration on page 106. Parts D and G are hardwood pieces cut earlier—they should be drilled as indicated, with a hole just big enough for the axle to turn easily. Drill a tiny lubricating hole through the top of D and G and mount those pieces on the frame (No. 8 flathead screws, 1½" long) so wheel is centered. Use a rasp to make depressions in the side of the frame so the wheel can fall into place and turn freely. The shank washer acts as a loose-fitting spacer, and the 0 ring as a soft washer between the flange and D. The hardwood piece that connects the axle to the treadle footman is drilled with a hole the same diameter as F. As you screw it on, threads are forced into the wood and the two pieces are held tightly. (Drill a test hole in a block of scrap first to be sure of a good tight fit.)

The Treadle. The illustrations show the treadle parts and the treadle installed. We made the plywood piece big enough so both feet could go on the treadle. Note that any thickness plywood would do—we felt 5/8" was esthetically pleasing, and it was handy. Form a channel in part No. 12 to fit over the iron rod. Notch it on the sides so it misses the frame as the treadle moves. Next, attach 2 and 3 to 1 with No. 8 screws, 1¼" long (7). The footman (4) is connected to 3 by a piece of leather that forms a flexible joint. Then slot the two wood pieces (¼" wide and 1⅛" deep). Bring a 1¼" roundhead bolt through the wood and the leather. A ¼" hexhead bolt, 2½" long, with two leather washers and a metal washer, joins the footman to the axle crank arm. The bolt slides through the footman and screws tightly into the hardwood. Take the bolt through a metal washer, a leather washer, the footman, a second leather washer, and then into the hardwood. You might have to adjust the length of 4 and the leather joint for smooth treadling.

Flyer and Bobbin. The harp-shaped part of the flyer starts out as shown in the illustration. Then part 2 is drilled through the center

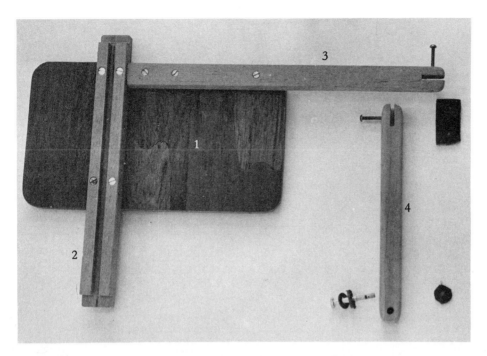

The treadle assembly as seen from underneath. Part 1 is ⅝" exterior plywood, 13 x 7". Pieces 2, 3, and 4 are fir. Part 2 is a 13" 1 x 2. Part 3 is a 15½" 1 x 1, and 4 is a 10" 1 x 1.

The treadle mechanism in place—the wheel should turn smoothly and effortlessly.

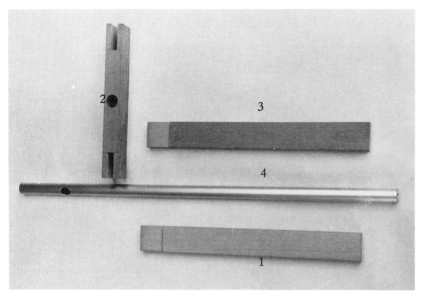

The basic flyer parts (the wood pieces are fir). Part 2 is a 9" 1 x 2; parts 1 and 3 are each 13½" 1 x 2's; part 4 is a 23" long aluminum tube with a ¾" outside diameter.

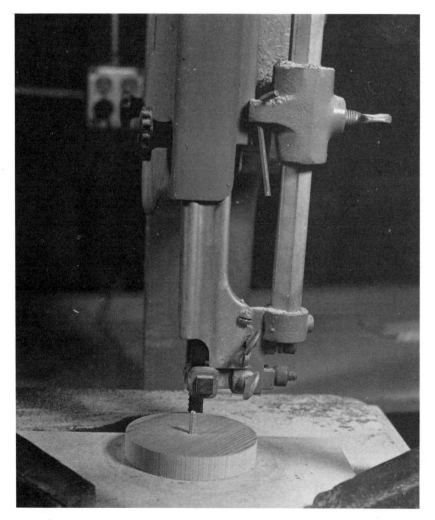

The bobbin ends shown in the next illustration are cut on the band saw in the same way the large wheel was cut—by turning it on a center axis.

to fit snugly over the metal tube. Slot part 2 at each end to allow it to receive notched sections of 1 and 3. Glue the dovetail, and shape the flyer by sanding to make it lighter and more graceful. Now screw in the cup hooks. Drill a hole in 4 approximately the same size as the inner diameter of the tube 3" from the end. Shape it and file it very smooth. The yarn will travel in through the open end of the tube for 3" and out through the second hole, angling up over the hooks on the flyer arm.

Before you anchor the flyer securely to the metal tube with a small brass screw (¾" long), finish the entire assembly, and put it on the spinning wheel. The spun yarn should travel through the hole and over the cup hooks at an angle that will create the least amount of friction, so make sure the flyer is in the proper position before anchoring it.

Use a file or rasp to form depressions in part 2. Those depressions lighten the flyer and allow the yarn—as it emerges from the hollow spindle—to travel with the greatest possible ease up over the cup hooks. The flyer should be balanced, so file and sand carefully. On some wheels, hooks are mounted on both flyer arms for balance, and, when staggered, help to distribute the yarn more evenly on the bobbin. The bobbin shaft (9) should fit just loosely enough over the metal spindle tube (4) to turn freely. The length of the bobbin shaft is important—the end should rest just beyond the flyer arms. Mount the bobbin pulley (11) in a vice, make a groove on the outer rim with a file, and then center and glue it to 10. Round the bobbin ends and drill the centers to fit snugly over 9.

Please note that the flyer and bobbin can be varied in a number

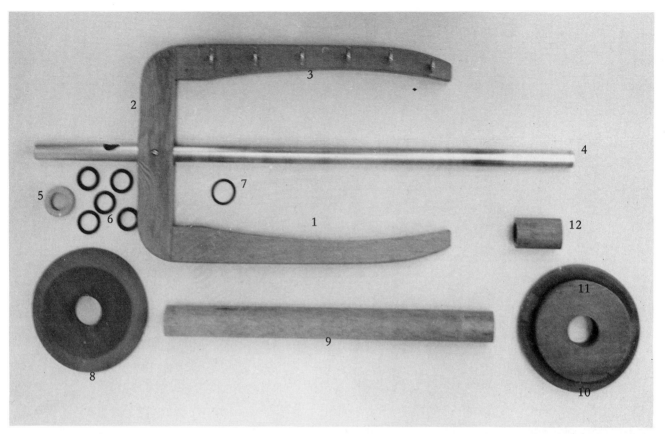

The basic flyer assembly (1, 2, 3, 4) is shown in position. Part 5 is 1½" long with an inside diameter of ¾" (masking tape could be substituted for this). Number 6 consists of five hose washers with ¾" inside diameters. Part 7 is a ⅞" O ring. Parts 8 and 10 are bobbin ends with a 5 ⅛" diameter, made from 1" thick redwood. Part 11 has a 4" diameter and is also made out of 1" redwood. The hollow shaft (9) that connects the ends is 14" long with a ⅞" inside diameter. Part 12 is like 9, but is a 2" length (5, 9, and 12 are all hollow ends of a window shade core).

The flyer and bobbin assembled and ready to slide into place on the spinning wheel frame.

A brake—made from a rubber band and a bit of seine twine—creates a drag on the flyer.

of ways. For example, the tube shafts can be smaller or larger or made of different materials.

The total flyer assembly and a description of the parts are shown on page 111. Read from front to back or from left to right. Parts 5 and 6 fit tightly, and act as spaces to hold 4 in position on the front maiden. A brake will drag on 5 and is shown on page 112. It could be made from tape or rubber. Part 7 fits loosely, and keeps the bobbin from rubbing against the flyer. Part 12 is a spacer between the bobbin and the back maiden that keeps the groove on 11 in line with the groove on the drive wheel.

Before the bobbin-flyer assembly can be dropped into place, the hardwood supports, or maidens, must be attached to the frame. The back maiden has a vertical slot that allows the flyer to be shifted up or down, which determines the amount of tension on the drive band. To maintain the vertical adjustment, use a 2½" bolt with a wing nut and at least one washer at each end. Anchor the front maiden from the inside with two No. 8 screws, 1" long. Fit the flyer on to the maidens. The metal tube slides into the back hole, and drops on to the front cradle. Adjust the back maiden to its lowest position, and bring the drive band under the large wheel and over the bobbin groove. Secure the ends so it fits snugly. We used a treadle sewing machine drive band that came with a staple for securing the ends, but any sturdy band that is not too smooth would work.

The Flyer Brake. The flyer brake is attached to the front maiden. It acts to dampen the speed of the flyer. To make it, screw a small eye into one side of the maiden and drill a hole all the way through on the other to accommodate a 2½" bolt with a double wing nut (two washers on each side). Half hitch a rubber band to the screw eye, and half hitch a piece of seine twine to the rubber band. Take the twine over the wood spacer on the flyer front, and clamp it securely between the two washers. The rubber band gives spring and elasticity, and avoids the need for frequent adjustment.

THE FINISHED WHEEL

The spinning wheel can be oiled, stained, or painted, or it can be left untouched. Rough spots and edges should be sanded.

The drive wheel should turn easily and be responsive to the treadle. If it has been properly centered, the drive wheel should track without wobbling. Lubricate with graphite, powdered teflon (clean), or even talcum powder those moving parts where metal and wood are in contact. In time, some of the hardwood parts may wear, especially if there are rough spots. This is most likely with the hardwood that holds the wheel axles. Pieces that have not been glued can always be replaced, of course. If the pieces have been glued, you can insert a sleeve of copper foil. It is also possible to drill the holes larger and insert teflon or nylon bearings or some other kind of bearing or bushing arrangement.

Happy Spinning

CHAPTER SIX

Fiber Preparation: Carding and Combing

She went up the mountain to pluck wild herbs;
She came down the mountain and met her former husband.
She knelt down and asked her former husband.
"What do you find your new wife like?"
"My new wife, although her talk is clever,
Cannot charm me as my old wife could.
But in usefulness they are not at all alike.
My new wife comes in from the road to meet me;
My old wife always came down from her tower.
My new wife weaves fancy silks;
My old wife was good at plain weaving.
Of fancy silk one can weave a strip a day;
Of plain weaving, more than fifty feet.
Putting her silks by the side of your weaving
I see that the new will not compare with the old."

Old and New, Anonymous, First Century A.D. Chinese

Teasing is a deliberate act, not just a nervous pulling. To tease wool, take a lock of fleece and hold it in your left hand, spreading it between thumb and fingers with the tips pointing toward you. Then, with your right hand, pull fibers out and away, and drop them in a pile off to the side.

The term fiber preparation is used here to refer to the rearrangement of fibers before spinning. The care and time spent in this preparation will affect your control of the forming yarn, the ease of spinning, the blending of color and fiber, and the smoothness of the spun yarn.

It might seem roundabout to present chapters discussing spinning on the hand spindle and on the spinning wheel before offering an explanation of fiber preparation techniques, but the methods discussed in this chapter will make more sense once you have some understanding of the principles of spinning. Many spinners need to give very little thought or energy to fiber preparation, since they prefer highly textured, irregular yarns or because they prefer and are able to purchase already prepared fibers. Perfect spinning and complete fiber preparation seem to go hand-in-hand, but for many purposes a perfect yarn is not necessarily the right yarn. In any case, though, learning about traditional methods of fiber preparation will help you understand the preparation process, whether that "perfect" fiber is to be bought in the rough or purchased fully prepared and ready to be spun.

Above all, fiber preparation requires time. In times past, the whole family was involved—long winter evenings were spent with everyone, even the young children, teasing and carding. There's an old saying that is appropriate. "It takes seven carders to keep one spinner going, and it takes seven spinners to keep one weaver going." You may ask why one should bother—why not just pay the extra money and buy fibers that are already prepared?

Generally speaking, fibers that are purchased prepared and ready for spinning have been put through a series of rigorous mechanical steps in preparation—not for the handspinner, but most often for spinning machines. The individual character and life that is part of the fiber is invariably sacrificed for uniformity. It is very much like the difference between fresh fruit and cooked fruit—some people like to pick an apple and eat it directly; others like to pick it, wash it, peel it, cut out the core, and cook it before eating. One way is not necessarily better than the other—it's just that there are many ways of eating an apple. So too, there are many ways of dealing with fibers.

The methods of fiber preparation discussed in this chapter are teasing, carding, and combing. They are discussed and demonstrated in relation to sheep's wool, but the same principles apply to other fibers. Other, more specialized or rarely used methods of preparing specific fibers are covered in the next two chapters. There are no rules for fiber preparation, just common sense guided by sight and touch.

TEASING

Teasing is the process of separating packed or matted fibers; it simply requires that the fibers be gently pulled apart and separated. As the fibers open up and separate, debris and short ends fall out. Teasing adds air and openness, or loft, to the fibers, so they will draw out smoothly in the spinning process. As the fibers separate, pick out the vegetable matter that won't shake loose. Animal fibers usually require both teasing and picking, since the natural oils attract dirt and debris, and keep the fibers packed. Some fibers, especially coarse ones, require little teasing; others require a great deal.

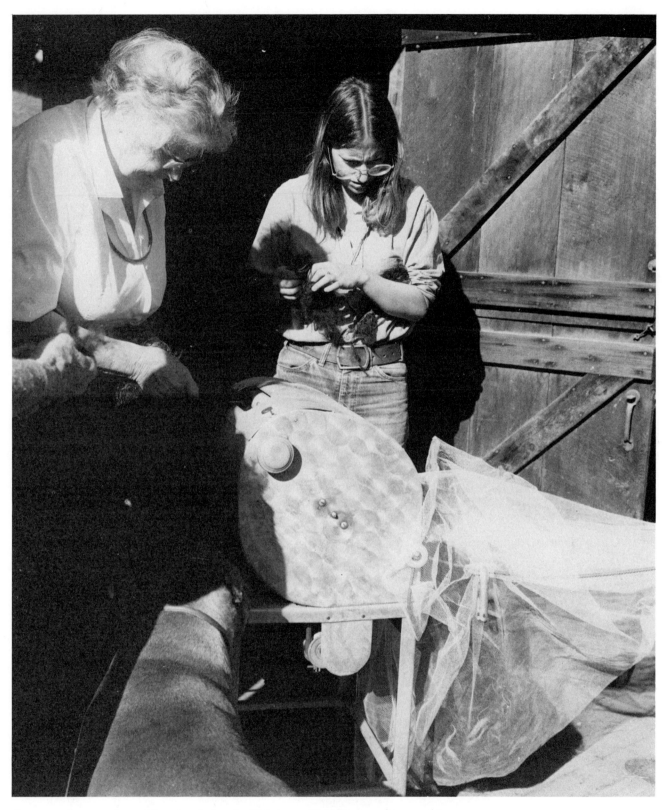

One never knows what might come in handy. This is an old picking machine used in the upholstery trade for tearing apart horse hair. Coarse, matted fibers that seem hopeless are literally ripped apart and shot out into a net basket.

These early California carders from the Spanish days are made of common thistles mounted between two slats. There is some question about whether they were used for carding fibers or for raising the nap on woven fabrics. (Photograph courtesy of the Oakland Museum.)

Hand carders are used in pairs. They come made of wood or metal, with either a flat or curved back. The setting of the teeth in the card-clothing varies depending on the fineness of the fibers to be carded. These are No. 8 wool cards. (Photograph by David Donoho.)

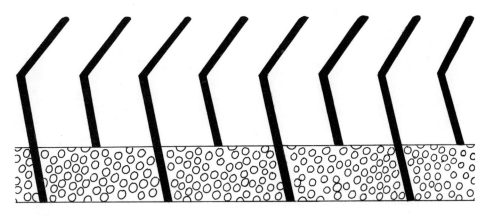

Card-clothing consists of sheets of material with symmetrical, staggered rows of slightly bent teeth that are actually the visible ends of U-shaped staples that penetrate the leather or composition cover from the underside. The staplelike arrangement prevents the teeth from pulling through and allows for flexibility. The spacing of the teeth is staggered to give an even all-over pull to the fibers. The teeth slant to hold fibers as the opposing set of teeth are drawn across, setting up the necessary tension for carding.

CARDING

Fibers are carded in much the same way that hair is brushed—loose, tangled fibers are made orderly. Thorough carding will later give you control over the forming yarn. It blends the fibers for color and texture, and contributes greatly to the opportunity for fine, even spinning. Fibers longer than 8" have a tendency to tangle in the carding process, and so are either cut for easy carding or combed.

Carding takes place when fibers are made to lie parallel after being brushed between two sets of flexible teeth. You can do this by hand either with a set of hand cards or with a drum carder. In the mills, this process is accomplished with large machines that contain a series of rollers covered with metal teeth; each successive roller has teeth set closer together, so a thorough carding—from rough to fine—results. The carded bat is then condensed by other machines into a perfectly uniform, continuous rope of arranged fibers, called a roving. The roving is ready to be spun on commercial spinning machines. Most fibers are available to the handspinner in this machine-prepared state.

Very early devices for carding fibers were made of thistles (teasles) mounted above a handle. Similar tools were used for raising the nap on finished textiles to give a brushed surface. The carders available today, though more practical than those using teasles, are similar to those used in preindustrial Europe. Each carder is a rectangular wood or metal piece with a handle. One side of the carder is covered with the card-clothing, traditionally a piece of leather perforated with wire teeth that bend slightly toward the handle. The carders work in pairs, and some spinners mark their cards with a "left" and "right" designation, since, as they wear, they will feel more comfortable being in the same hand all the time. Carders with finely spaced teeth are used for carding fine fibers; those with heavy, widely spaced teeth for coarse fibers or for use in the initial carding of finer fibers. Carders themselves, by the way, can be cleaned with a metal comb and brush.

CARDING WITH HAND CARDS

This is the most basic way of carding.

Step 1. Sit down and rest the left carder, teeth up, on your lap so the handle points to your left. Begin by taking teased fibers and spreading them over the teeth. To do this, catch the fibers on the teeth near the handle edge, and, with your fingers, draw them straight across until they cover most of the toothed surface. This process is

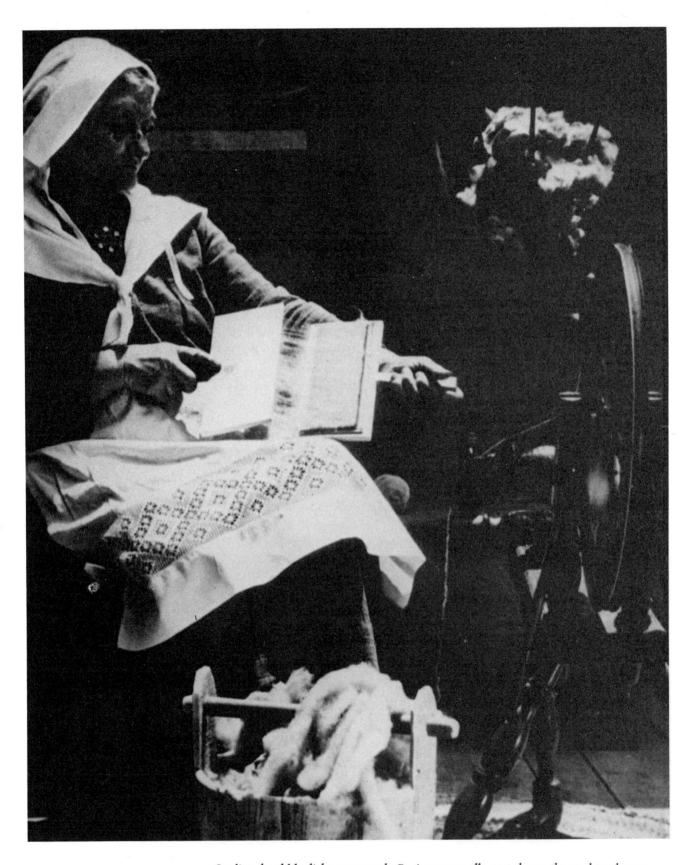

Carding should be light, easy work. Beginners usually overcharge the cards and press too hard as they brush. Work for a thin, uniform batt, and don't allow the teeth to touch when brushing. Be patient—it takes time to break in a new pair of carders and to develop a comfortable style. (Photograph from a lantern slide, courtesy of J. and S. Zarbaugh.)

called "charging." If you are working with unwashed wool fibers, put a cloth underneath to catch the dirt and debris.

Step 2. Hold the charged card steady with the left hand, and draw the right card lightly across so the teeth brush and straighten the fibers. During this movement, the teeth slant in opposing directions, and the right card is drawn across to the right, lifted, placed back on the left carder, and drawn across until the fibers are brushed straight. Carding should be light and easy—too much pressure will cause the teeth to lock and hold. Card the fibers, not the cards. A sort of patting motion can be made with the right card to lift the fibers to the surface. Please note that as you draw the right carder across, some of the fibers will catch and shift to the upper carder. These fibers should be periodically transferred back to the bottom carder.

Step 3. Transfer the fibers back to the left card by taking the top edge (the edge opposite the handle) of the right carder and placing it at the bottom edge of the left carder. Push the right carder across the left so the fibers are again on the left carder. To do this smoothly, the left carder must be lifted and turned slightly. Otherwise, it will feel awkward.

Step 4. Continue brushing and transferring until the fibers are even and uniform. Then remove the straightened fibers (called a batt) in a quick, tricky motion. Transfer the fibers to the left carder as described in Step 3, and then quickly bring the right carder back down (the exact reverse motion) as if you were going to peel the fibers off the left carder. This releases the batt of carded fibers, which can be left flat or rolled in the short direction to form a rolag. Rolag is a Scandi-

Wool fibers at various stages of preparation. On the top left is a lock of wool from a freshly shorn sheep's fleece; top right are the teased fibers; in the center is the carded batt that has been lifted from the hand carder; and on the bottom is the carded batt rolled into a rolag.

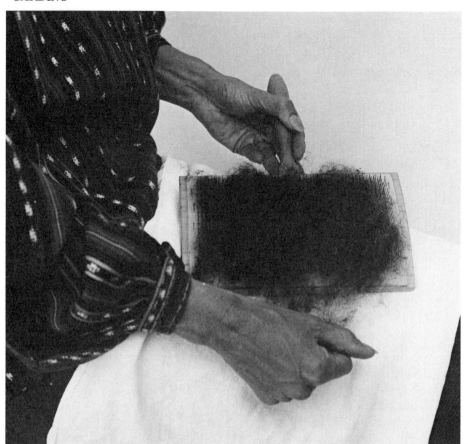

Step 1. Spread fibers that have been completely teased over the teeth of one carder.

Step 2. Draw the second carder lightly over the first from left to right; lift and repeat until the fibers are evenly brushed.

Step 3. Transfer the fibers that were picked up by the second carder back to the first.

Step 4. Brush and transfer until the fiber batt is even and uniform. Then release the fibers from the first card by teeth action (or lift with fingers), and roll into a rolag.

navian word that means "rolled air." Spinning begins from the end of this light, airy roll of aligned fibers.

CARDING ON THE DRUM CARDING MACHINE

The drum carder is a more complex piece of hand equipment than hand carders and is favored by many handspinners for carding because it is faster than, although usually not as thorough as, the hand carders. There are different models now available for purchase, but they function in much the same way. On most machines, there are two rollers, one large and one small, each covered with the card-clothing. A drive band or chain connects the two rollers or drums.

Step 1. Place a small mass of teased fibers on the tray near the small roller, and turn the hand crank clockwise. The teeth on the small roller catch the fibers and draw them under and around to meet the teeth of the large drum. As the two drums pass, the fibers are drawn on to and around the large roller. It is at this point that carding occurs. Keep feeding in small amounts of teased fibers so the carded batt fills up evenly on the large roller.

Step 2. Find the place on the large drum where the ends of the card-clothing join to create a wide space without teeth. Take a long, sturdy, pointed rod—such as a knitting needle or ice pick—and slide it along the join and underneath the batt. Lift up, pulling the fibers until they separate. Maintaining fiber length is important, so scissors should not be used. Pull the batt off the drum as you turn the crank counterclockwise. The batt can be rolled to form a rolag, which in turn can be drawn out and then

The drum carding machine works on the same principle as the hand carders: the interaction of opposing sets of angled teeth. There are, however, certain adjustments that must be made for it to work properly. The teeth of the small roller should just barely touch the edge of the metal pan, and the teeth between the two rollers should not quite touch, although they should be parallel. The drive belt (far side) that runs between the two rollers must be tight enough for good friction, and the carding machine should be oiled occasionally in the holes provided. (Photograph by David Donoho.)

Step 1. Place small amounts of teased fibers on the metal tray near the small roller, and turn the crank clockwise to draw them in. If the fibers are properly teased, they will transfer to the big drum and not wind around the small roller. If too many fibers are fed in at one time, the crank will be difficult to turn and undue pressure will be exerted on the card-clothing.

Step 2. Separate the carded fibers, and peel off the carded batt. If you are working with unwashed greasy wool, there will inevitably be a build-up of miscellaneous fibers and debris on both rollers. This can be removed by prying with a thin wire. On the table near the carding machine are a pair of antique wool combs.

spun. A flat carded batt can be formed into a soft rope called a card sliver by separating the batt from long end to long end in a zig-zag fashion.

THE FLICK CARDER

This small and inexpensive tool, similar to a cat brush but with wider spaced teeth, is sometimes used on longer fibers. The flick carder works exactly as a brush does. Take a lock of fleece, hold it on a padded surface, and brush the fibers as you would your hair. Then turn the lock around, and brush the other end, until the fibers are ready for spinning.

CARDING DEVICES

The various carding devices are tools that may be used in traditional ways, and in ways that are unique to the fiber worker. They can be used not only to make up rolags, but also to blend different colors and different kinds or lengths of fibers into combinations that produce richly varied, one-of-a-kind yarns. Carded batts can be divided and recarded for layering or to increase blending or to further align the fibers. Some spinners do not card at all; others card only in a cursory fashion to merely put fibers in order for fast spinning; still others card, and recard, examining and comparing every square inch for uniformity and order. Carding can be what you wish it to be, and, when used with care and imagination, carding tools may bring many effects to be spun yarn that would—without their help—be difficult to achieve.

COMBING

Fibers that are carded tend to produce fuzzy, soft, airy, or lofty yarns. Longer fibers, though, are

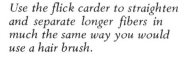

Use the flick carder to straighten and separate longer fibers in much the same way you would use a hair brush.

sometimes combed rather than carded to produce dense, smooth, lustrous yarns. Combing is the process of drawing fibers through rigid teeth in order to align and straighten the elements longitudinally. Combing pulls the fibers straight and parallel, and separates out the short fibers, called noils. The process is much like the combing of human hair—tangles and snarls must be worked out. Combing begins at the tips and progresses toward the base, and the fibers become freer and fluffier as work goes on. Like carding, combing can be as simple or as complex a procedure as you wish. Some spinners prefer to spend the time and energy necessary to align all the fibers perfectly, while others—more hurried or seeking a less smooth product—do a less complete job.

The equipment necessary for combing will vary, but usable combs—depending on the fiber and its condition—might include those designed originally for use with human or pet hair. Most commonly, fibers are pulled through a comb that is attached to some substantial base. The pulling can be done either by hand or with another comb. Large, long-tined wool combs, like the North European set shown in the illustration at right are used in pairs. One comb is anchored to a post or table, and the other held in the hands. These large heavy combs make it easier to deal with thick, heavy fibers and fiber clusters.

The fibers are sometimes moistened and oiled to protect them from breaking in the combing process. In preindustrial Europe, the combs were actually kept warm on charcoal stoves to keep the oil from sticking. This greatly facilitated combing. Most contemporary spinners will find that a comfortable chair before a stove or

In pre-industrial Europe, wool combing was traditionally done with a set of combs, each with two or three rows of very long steel teeth. The combs were first heated, and then one was fitted horizontally on to a support anchored in a post. This comb was loaded with clean, moistened, and oiled wool that was kept readily available in nearby tubs. The second comb was then taken in both hands and the tines were brought straight down through the fibers, beginning at the tips and gradually moving upward toward the anchored comb. The combs were periodically heated to keep the oil flowing. Gradually the wool was "fetched" off the anchored comb on to the free comb, and then, by shifting the position of the free comb, worked back on to the anchored comb. (A Diderot Pictorial Encyclopedia of Trades and Industry.)

A pair of contemporary North European wool combs with a special clamp for securing one to a post or table. Long wool fibers, such as these from the Spelsau sheep, can be combed to separate the long outer hairs from the short inner hairs.

These Icelandic wool combs, similar to those used by Scandinavian wool combers for centuries, are used for coarse fibers. (Photograph by Jackie Wollenberg.)

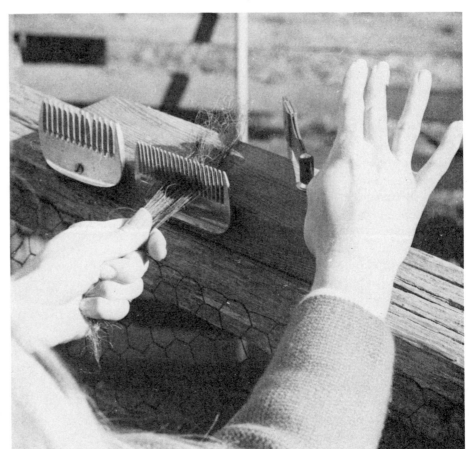

Satisfactory combs can be made easily by mounting metal animal combs on a block of wood and then clamping the wood to a railing or table. Small groups of fibers can be quickly drawn through the tines.

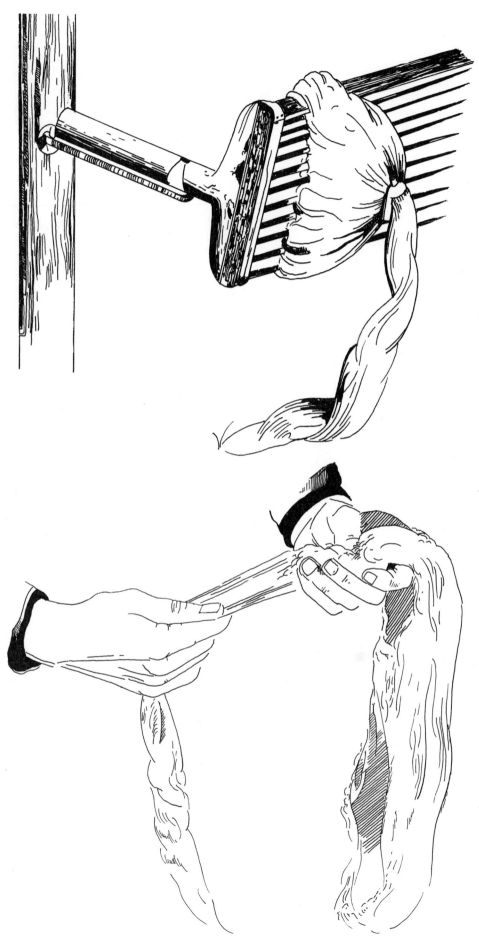

Traditionally, after the second combing, the fibers were drawn off through a horn "diz" that reduced the size and bulk of the roving (or sliver), which was then wound into a wad called a "top."

Many spinners prefer to create a roving or sliver only slightly thicker than the yarn they plan to spin. Just before spinning, combed or carded fibers can be divided into thinner sections or drawn out between the hand. The reduced diameter of the fiber arrangement allows for easier spinning.

Dont eat a dont abuse not sell sell animals

fireplace, or simply a warm day, will do the trick.

WOOLEN AND WORSTED

Woolen and worsted refer to the kinds of wool yarns that are spun using carded and combed fibers respectively. Carded batts or rolags contain short fibers that inevitably lie in varying directions. This makes woolen yarns, which are composed of carded fibers, airy and somewhat fuzzy.

In the fiber industry, wool fibers that are to be combed are sometimes carded first. Combing then removes all the short fibers, straightens them, and puts them in a close parallel order. The resulting rope of combed fibers is condensed into a thinner arrangement, called a sliver, and wound into a ball called a top. Combed top is then spun into crisp, smooth-surfaced yarns called worsted. Worsted spinning usually produces hard twist, strong, lustrous yarns that are relatively nonelastic.

During fiber preparation, no matter what the fiber, the hand-spinner can influence the ultimate yarn by emphasizing either the woolen or the worsted concept.

This drawing shows the difference between a woolen and a worsted yarn—the woolen yarn is an orderly tangle of short carded fibers, while the worsted yarn is composed of long fibers combed parallel.

Come all ye master combers, and hear of our Big Ben,
He'll comb more wool in one day than fifty of your men,
With their hand-combs and comb-pots, and such old fashioned ways,
There'll be no more occasion for old Bishop Blaize.

Big Ben was made at Doncaster, that place of great renown,
And is a noble fellow, supported by the Crown;
Whenever you shall see him he'll put you in amaze,
And make you praise the inventor, our new Bishop Blaize.

Our triumph then this day there's nothing shall prevent,
For know, our great mechanic by Providence was set
For the good of mankind, boys—a trophy then we'll raise
To our British Archimedes, our new Bishop Blaize.

The hungry he gives bread to; the naked, too, he clothes;
Thy health and joy and riches attend him as he goes;
Then fill you glasses high, boys! and give three huzzas:
Here's our good and worthy master—our new Bishop Blaize!

Bishop Blaize was supposedly tortured to death by wool combs as shown in this drawing taken from a sixteenth century Italian illustration. All long, stapled wool used in spinning worsted yarn was still combed by hand until 1790. The English wool combers were a well paid, highly organized, and very colorful, independent group. Theirs was one of the last textile occupations to be mechanized by the industrial revolution. The Reverend Edmund Cartwright invented a wool combing machine in the early 1790s (referred to as "Big Ben" after a popular prize fighter); Cartwright immediately became—to the wool combers—"the new Bishop Blaize." To be cast in such a questionable role was not new to Cartwright, who had earlier perfected the power loom, an invention that did not endear him to the handweavers. Many admired his genius, however, which was acknowledged in this little verse above, sung to him by his workers at a party in Doncaster (from Wool Knowledge: The Journal of Wool Education*).*

CHAPTER SEVEN

Wool and Other Animal Fibers

Not greed nor gold nor gad-
getry, nor principalities nor
powers, including all the com-
bined resources of the artificial fibre industry have been
able to synthesize a single
solitary strand of wool.

The Web, August 1974

A primitive, rugged sheep found in the Faeroe Islands, between Iceland and Norway. This type of sheep was brought from the coast of Norway to these islands during Viking times. (Photograph by Jackie Wollenberg.)

Animal fibers, primarily those that grow on domesticated sheep, offer the handspinner a fine source of fibers for spinning. The emphasis here is on sheep's wool because it is especially easy and enjoyable to spin, readily available in various qualities and forms, and relatively inexpensive. Many animals are thought of and classified as wool-bearers, but only domestic sheep grow true wool. Their covering, or fleece, is a mass of fibers growing from the sheep's body in groups, or locks. The density, length, and fineness vary considerably from breed to breed. Other animal fibers are similar to sheep's wool in general physical and chemical properties, but their availability is limited, and the yarns produced are not as varied or useful.

This chapter begins with the general characteristics of animal fibers, followed by an examination of the range of those fibers traditionally used in spinning. Although the major part of the material presented deals with sheep's wool, most of the practical information can be applied to the treatment and use of other animal fibers. Those other, so-called specialty, fibers—such as mohair, cashmere, and alpaca—are usually available to the handspinner through supply houses and give special pleasure through their softness, rarity, and unique characteristics.

GENERAL CHARACTERISTICS

Animal fibers are composed of protein. Like human hairs, they are the products of animal growth in the form of a protective coating. They can be damaged by light, bleach, alkali, and—especially with sheep's wool—by moths. Generally speaking, yarns spun from animal fibers have elasticity and resilience, have good insulating qualities, and dye easily. They are in their weakest stage when wet, and should always be treated with special care during washing and drying procedures. Also strong alkali soaps will damage the fibers and should not be used. Note too that protein fibers are naturally fire resistant; they do not burn quickly and are self-extinguishing.

Within each animal fiber type, there is tremendous quality variation, which will affect decisions concerning methods used in handling and spinning—the fibers will determine the kind and use of yarn produced. The only way to really judge quality, other than by dealing with a reputable, knowledgeable source, is by sight and feel—always use your finger tips and common sense when selecting fibers. Your plans for the fibers should be the influencing factor. Fine, short fibers spin into thin, soft yarns; coarse, long fibers will spin into textured, heavy yarns.

Some spinners have been concerned enough about their choice of fiber characteristics that they breed and raise their own sheep. Such fully committed spinners are able to take advantage of the inherent differences, not only of a particular breed of animal, but also the differences within each individual fleece, to spin a specific fiber for a specific yarn for a specific need. Anne Blinks, who raises black sheep for her own use and for sale, speaks with patience of "people who write and say they want a fleece, but don't say what wool characteristics they are looking for." Since each animal and each fleece is unique, it is difficult for the wool supplier to know what to send if requests are not specific. Since the variety of the characteristics in the wool of different breeds of sheep is great, and since the variation of characteristics within an individual fleece is sometimes considerable, it is really only through experience that the handspinner gains a feel for fibers and how to handle them. The tremendous range available in sheep's wool, although confusing at first, offers a pleasing variety to the person with the energy, interest, and time to pursue spinning.

SHEEP'S WOOL

Wool is one of the oldest and most universally used textile fibers. The sheep offered food and clothing and was—and still is—for many people an animal close to the heart and to the pocketbook. Since Roman days, selective breeding has produced a wide assortment of sheep that have adapted to almost every climatic and geographical condition.

The early, wild, primitive mountain sheep had a double coat of wool, a long hairy outer coat of coarse fibers, and a downy under coat of soft, short fibers. Some breeds of sheep today, such as the Karakul, retain this double coat. It is also found in other animals, such as the cashmere goat, the musk oxen, and some dogs. Sheep's wool, though, has particular characteristics that make it especially suitable for spinning.

Like the hairs on humans, wool fibers grow from follicles in the skin. Depending on the breed and the frequency of shearing, the fibers range in length from 1 to 20"—lengths from 3 to 6" are ideal for spinning. Structurally, each fiber is composed of three layers; an outer layer of overlapping scales; a middle layer, the cortex; and a central core, or medula. This central core is sometimes lacking in very fine wool fibers. The surface

These sheep, bred by Anne Blinks, represent a Corriedale-Lincoln cross. Anne has been raising and breeding black sheep for 18 years. She was led to sheep breeding through her interest in ancient textiles.

That are idiotic lies, its recreation = creation by GOD ISRAEL against all evil, in his GOD ISRAEL Total laws! Its not breeding, they don't breed on any kind!

135

In Blaxhall, Suffolk, England, a small cottage known to the older local inhabitants as Smugglers' Cottage stands even now—it used to be used, it is believed, to store contraband brought there by Liney Richardson, a shepherd-smuggler who flourished in the mid-nineteenth century. Liney, who was widely admired for his understanding of the best ways to treat sick or injured sheep, was admired too for his night-time operation, where he would "borrow" a team and wagon from a not unwilling—and admirably rewarded—local farmer. In the morning the team would be back in their stalls, with perhaps a keg or two of the contraband also tucked into the stable. The bulk of the illegal stuff would be hidden in the Smugglers' Cottage, and the road, likely to be inspected by the tax men looking for wagon tracks, would show only the marks of sheep—Liney's sheep—which had been herded close behind the contraband-carrying wagon in order to cover the signs of their owner's second occupation.

When viewed under the microscope, a wool fiber appears as a cylindrical tapered tube with surface scales pointing and overlapping toward the tip. There are many more scales on a fine fiber than on a coarse fiber. Those scales break up the surface and refract light, accounting for the lack of luster in short, fine-wool fibers.

scales, which overlap pointing toward the tip of the fiber, give wool its unique binding quality. These scales allow wool fibers to catch and hold one another, and this catching and holding greatly facilitates spinning—the fibers are twisted into yarn, and the scale structure creates air pockets, so wool forms a light, springy yarn. Fine fibers, which are invariably short, have a high concentration of scales and produce soft, woolly yarns. Longer fibers, which are coarser, have fewer and flatter scales, and consequently spin into smoother, firmer, more lustrous yarns. These overlapping scales vary from 24,000 to the inch in fine fibers, to half that number in the coarser forms.

When the scales protrude, as they do in fine wools, felting occurs very easily. The tendency toward felting is an important quality of wool. When the fibers are subjected to water, and especially to hot water, the scales open and expand as the fiber absorbs water. If there is agitation or a sudden temperature change, the scales become permanently interlocked and felting occurs. Felting is increased by treatment with acids or alkaline solutions as well as with boiling water. This means that strong soaps should not be used on wool and that wool fibers, especially fine ones, must be handled carefully when wet. However, a certain amount of felting is desirable and considered part of the finishing treatment for wool fabrics. Note that wool fibers can become felted into a solid mass whether spun or unspun.

The wool fiber also has a natural crimp, or wave, which goes up and down the fiber as well as from side to side. The intensity of the crimp varies from sheep to sheep, from being very fine and close in short fibers to broad and wavy in long, coarse fibers. The crimp often resembles the results of a tight permanent wave. It is a result of unevenly arranged structural differences within the fiber, contributes to the elasticity and resiliency of wool fibers, and acts with the scales to hold and trap air. While on the sheep, each wool fiber is protected from injury and from matting or felting by a gland in the skin that produces a grease (lanolin) that coats the fiber. This grease holds in sweat, dirt, and burrs, and sometimes congeals to lock the fibers together. Most handspinners purchase their fleece "in the grease," still containing the natural grease or lanolin as well as the sweat, dirt, and other impurities attracted and held by the grease. This dirt amounts to from 30 to 60% of the total weight of the wool. The wool fibers can be spun while still greasy, or they can be washed and scoured first. The grease adds to the cohesiveness of the fibers, though, so wool "in the grease" is preferred by many spinners.

BREEDS OF SHEEP

Fleeces from many breeds of sheep are available to the handspinner, and, since the choice is so broad, attempts to choose the proper wool can be bewildering. Although the best way to select is by looking and feeling, some general information about breeds might be helpful. In some breeds, the quality of the wool has been totally ignored and the sheep bred and raised for meat. For many farmers, the sheep's fleece is nothing but an annoyance. Fleece from such a sheep will generally be short, coarse, dirty, and unattractive. The handspinner is interested in quality fleece, so this short, rough fleece is of little value or interest.

Sheep breeds are divided into four basic groups: long-wooled, medium-wooled, down breeds, and fine-wooled. As mentioned earlier, long-wooled sheep produce coarse fleece. The long-wooled sheep are descendents of lowland breeds and produce long, lustrous fibers with a wavy or wide crimp. These fibers are widely used in the carpet in-

The Lincoln Longwool carries a heavy-luster fleece with a length of 12 to 16". The wool is coarse, and the breed is frequently crossed with finer-wooled sheep to increase length and luster.

The Suffolk is a hornless, long-bodied sheep with a black face and legs. The fleece has a staple length of 2 to 3" and has been used since the Middle Ages for wool fabrics. The Suffolk is mainly bred today as a meat sheep with little attention paid to the fleece.

137

dustry and are frequently favored by spinners who want to spin sturdy, tight twist yarns. Long-wooled sheep breeds include Lincoln, Romney Marsh, and Cotswold.

Fleece from medium-wooled sheep usually has good luster and excellent spinning qualities, but not the length of the long-wooled breeds. Cheviot and Corriedale are medium-wooled sheep. The down breeds have short, spongy coats, and are of little interest to the handspinner. Southdown and Suffolk (found widely in California) are two such breeds. Their fleece lacks character, and they are usually bred for mutton.

sheep and are strong favorites among most spinners. The Corriedale sheep was developed in the late nineteenth century in Scotland, a cross of New Zealand Merino ewes and Lincoln rams. It is now a popular sheep in the United States. The Corriedale produces a heavy, dense, open fleece, and the fibers are easy to handle, have lots of crimp and character, and will produce a variety of yarns.

Another favorite, especially among those spinners seeking textured yarns with lots of natural color variation, is the Karakul, an ancient breed that still retains the double coat of primitive mountain sheep. Its native home is

Merino sheep were important enough to the economy of Spain that a special court, or "mesta," convened each year in Madrid to maintain, establish, and enforce the many rules and traditions that governed the breeding, care, and use of the Merino sheep. The king himself was the patron of Merino breeders. Today the Merino is considered to be the producer of the finest wool generally available, and there is a bit—and in many cases more than just a bit—of Merino blood in most other domesticated breeds.

The fine-wooled sheep, which include Merino and Ramboulliet, are descendants of mountain sheep. The course outer guard hairs were bred out long ago as the fine quality soft fibers were bred in. The fleece from the pure Merino, developed by the Spanish in the fourteenth century, is very fine and highly crimped, but it is difficult to deal with, felts very easily, and can be very frustrating for the beginner. Much time and care must be spent in preparing the Merino fibers for spinning. Because of its fine fleece, the Merino has been crossed with many other kinds of sheep to improve fleece quality. Romney Marsh and Corriedale are two such

Bokhara, in west central Asia. The animal has a flat, broad tail which stores fat; this excess fat allows the animal to survive long periods with little food. Generally, the wool is clean, long, coarse, and wavy, with the best fleece coming from the younger animals. The double coat can be separated by combing, or the two parts can be spun together to produce variegated, highly textured yarns. As with other primitive sheep that have not gone through intensive selective breeding, the black color is dominant in Karakuls. Note that any sheep that is not white is considered black, and black fleece frequently exhibits the whole range of natural colors from pale gray to jet black, including various shades of brown. Many farmers or spinners who raise black sheep avoid the Karakul because it has poor herding qualities, coarse hair which becomes very coarse and faded with age, and a sometimes disagreeable temperament. Since there are very few pure Karakuls available, most stock has so many differences that breeding is a hit and miss operation. The fleece of the unborn Karakul lambs—very tightly curled and often in a beautiful or interesting pattern—are still used, mostly in Asia, for hats and coats. Unfortunately, the tight curls open up, and the patterns begin to fade as soon

sheep was rigidly eliminated from flocks. A black sheep was considered an indication of poor breeding and was a general embarrassment. Now a good black fleece brings a premium price. The long emphasis on white had to do with the need for color control among commercial users—for standardized dyeing, a white base is necessary.

SPINNING COUNT

The fineness or coarseness of wool is identified in the trade by its hypothetical spinning count. This number is frequently mentioned in relation to breeds of sheep and is a good indicator to the handspinner of the yarn that can be spun from

The voyages of Columbus and the Conquistadors were financed largely by income from the wool trade. For obvious reasons, Spain guarded this source of wealth closely and prohibited, under penalty of death, the exportation of even one ewe. In 1786, though, Louis XVI of France was able to import 386 Merino ewes from Spain, and crossed them with other sheep on his estate at Rambouillet. The result of this cross was a new breed, Rambouillet, still one of the most desirable of the sheep breeds.

as the animal is born.

Generally speaking, the finer the wool, the more crimp, and the shorter the staple, or length, of the fibers. Fine wool is very soft and will spin into a fine thread. The fine wools come from the so-called range breeds of sheep, which are always white-faced sheep. According to the general rule, the finer the wool the greater the herd instinct, so it is possible to raise these range breeds in open areas with relatively little supervision. Black-faced sheep have little herd instinct and must be confined. Although a great deal of interest has been shown toward black fleece lately, until very recently the black

the fleece. This grading scale of one to one hundred indicates the relative fineness found within a breed, and from breed to breed. The count is determined by the number of hanks, each 560 yards long, that can be machine spun from 1 pound of clean fibers. The finer the wool, the thinner the thread. A count in the 70s and above is considered superfine. Medium wools are ranked in the 50s and 60s, with coarse wools on the lower end of the scale in the 20s and 30s. The fleece from the full-blooded Merino sheep would typically be upwards of the 70s, while the long, shiny locks of the Lincoln would be in the 30s.

The fleece grows as a dense, deep coat surrounding the sheep. This black fleece, still on the back of the animal, is spread to show the length and quality of the fibers. Many years of breeding have gone into achieving this open, lustrous, black fleece.

(Below) Sheep's wool can vary greatly in length, texture, and crimp from breed to breed. On the left are the long coarse fibers of the Herdwick. Moving to the right are the shorter fibers of the Shetland breed on top and those of the Gotland below. Next are long dark-tipped curls of the Spelsau; on the top right Cheviot; and on the bottom Jacob.

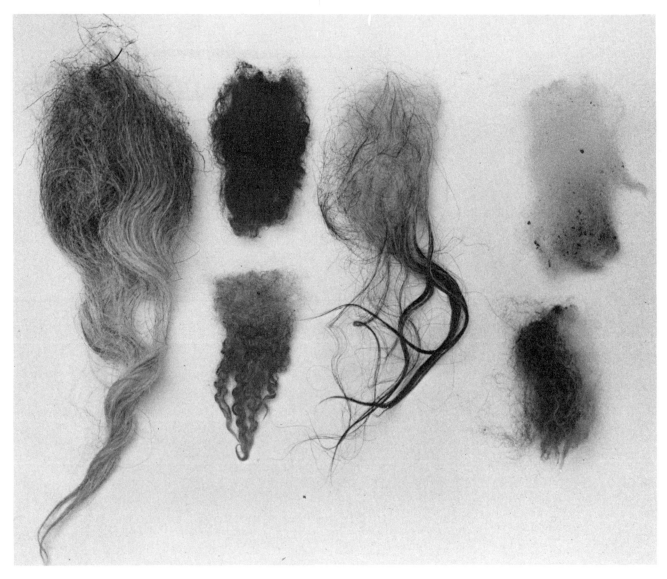

Books listed in the bibliography deal specifically with breeds of sheep. These can be very helpful to the handspinner when confronted with the fleece of an unfamiliar breed.

SELECTING A FLEECE

Knowing the breed and the spinning count tells the spinner a great deal about what to expect from a fleece. But this is still only the beginning. Many people with small flocks, and most people who raise black sheep, are continually trying to improve their flocks. They are not necessarily working to maintain a full-blood line or breed, but they are constantly crossing to come up with a sheep that they can live with and that will produce a particular color, a particular length of fiber, and a particular feel. Some breeds are temperamental; some need special protection; some won't cross-breed; and so on. For instance, the Cheviot is a popular breed due to its good all-round fleece for spinning and its manageability and adaptability. The following almost affectionate excerpt from *Scottish Woolens* reflects feelings frequently held and commented on by those who raise them. "The Cheviot, let it be said to its eternal credit, is a contented sheep—that is, it will readily adapt itself to circumstances, and by keeping its mind easy will thrive under adverse conditions—a lesson to humanity."

Sheep are sheared once or twice a year with hand clippers or, more usually, with electric shears. Shearing is hard work, and a good shearer (who doesn't cut the sheep or have to make second cuts while removing a fleece) is not easy to find, especially for the owner of a small flock. The well-cut fleece is clipped from the animal and falls off in one piece of loosely connected locks of fibers. A fine fleece will usually weigh from 2 to 8 pounds; a coarser fleece from 6 to 15 pounds. The fleece, still containing all the grease and dirt, is then folded and rolled into a bundle, with the clean, or flesh, side out. It is not always possible for the purchaser to unroll the fleece and look at the entire coat, but there are certain factors that can help in making a decision. The age of the animal will have a bearing on the quality of the fleece—the first

Simple hand clippers are still used to shear sheep in places where there is no access to electricity or when traditional tools are preferred.

A curious difference in the habits of the Merino and Cheviot sheep is worth noting. In a flock of Cheviots you find that the sheep range apart in twos and threes, but the Merinos keep together like a drove passing through the country. They form a sort of camp at night, and nothing will induce them to "lie abroad," as the shepherds call sleeping on their own particular bit of ground, like other mountain breeds. The second of these traits manifests itself in the cross, but curiously enough not the first. So you find a Cheviot sheep, with a strong strain of Merino in it, feeding apart during the day, but returning at night to camp with its fellows. It can easily be appreciated that on a large hirsel of several thousand acres an individual sheep that has chosen the outlying ground has a considerable journey to make both morning and evening.

Scottish Woollens, p. 67

A full Gotland fleece as it came from the animal. Usually after a sheep is sheared the fleece is folded and rolled into a bundle, skin side out. Sometimes the fleece can be unrolled, still in the shape of the animal.

shearing of a sheep is called the lamb's fleece and is the softest, finest fleece the animal will produce. The second shearing is considered the best. Breeds differ, and some produce a good, high-quality fleece for many years, but usually there is a falling off in quantity and fineness after the third year. The factors to look for when given a choice between many bundles or parts of fleece are listed below.

Cleanliness. Cleanliness is a very important factor. In some instances, sheep are washed and groomed before shearing. Very simple things can make an enormous difference, such as whether the floor was swept before the greasy fleece landed on it, or whether the sheep spent its last six months rolling on green grass or in dirt full of plant debris. Such factors will have a tremendous influence over whether you will want the fleece or not. Logically, wool from wet areas tends to be cleaner. This is why, among other reasons, fleece from New Zealand is so popular among handspinners. In California and the American Southwest, where there are long

dry spells, the local fleeces can be very dirty.

The buyer of a dirty fleece not only pays for the dirt, dung, and debris that comes with the fibers, but also "pays" later in the time required for extensive washing and handpicking of excess debris. Cleanliness is easily judged by sight and feel. A fine fleece has more natural grease and will have a tendency to be dirtier than a coarse fleece, other things being equal. As mentioned above, grease, dirt, and debris can account for as much as 30 to 60% of the total fleece weight.

Openness. The openness of the fleece is another quality of major importance to the handspinner. In order to spin, fibers must be able to slide past one another, and preparation for this requires them to be pulled apart. If the fleece is open, the locks of wool will pull apart easily, but sometimes the grease will congeal or the fibers actually mat, making it very difficult to separate the fibers. I once received a fleece that was so matted that I couldn't even cut it apart with scissors. Don't be seduced by beautiful color or nice curls—a fleece that won't part easily is not worth bothering with.

Fiber length. Fiber length facilitates spinning up to a certain point. Fibers between 3 and 6" in length are the easiest to spin, while shorter and longer fibers require more preparation and skill.

Fiber soundness. It is also important to check for fiber soundness. One way to do so is to take a small group of fibers, stretch them out between your hands, and, while grasping the two ends, snap the fibers in an attempt to break them. Weak spots will give and break, and such weakness will probably run throughout the entire fleece. Sometimes, particularly in black sheep, the locks will have burnt tips that are matted together. These discolored or matted tips can be cut off if the color or damage interferes with preparation or spinning.

Crimp, color, luster. The amount of crimp and the luster, or sheen, will vary depending on the fineness or coarseness of the fleece, but these factors should be uniform throughout any one fleece. Color is an individual preference. Remember, though, that no matter how clean the fleece looks, there is very likely to be a considerable amount of dirt which obscures both the color and the luster.

Handle. The general handle, or feel, of the fleece should be springy and lively. The fiber formations should be free and airy, and the lanolin or grease moist and sparkly. The fibers should be beautiful to hold and to behold.

CLEANING: SORTING, WASHING, AND SCORING

After obtaining a fleece, the first step is to unroll it on a clean floor, table, or lawn. The unrolled fleece should take the form of the animal, with the back sides in the middle and the legs extending outward. As you handle the greasy fleece, bits of dirt and debris will fall out, so try to handle the fibers in such a way that the dirt and debris do not get back in. Remember, even a "clean," but unwashed, fleece is dirty. The rear end is likely to be full of dung, and the neck section will sometimes be stretched out. After shearing, when the fleece is rolled, this stretched part wraps around and secures the bundle.

The first step is to skirt the fleece. Many people who raise sheep for their wool do this right after shearing. It is a matter of taking off the dirty, unusable fibers from around the edge. This usually includes the belly wool, which is frequently short, soft, and dense. This process leaves the best and cleanest part of the fleece for spinning, and the "tags" can be used in the garden as compost. In some breeds, the fleece will vary enough from one part to another in fiber quality or color that the spinner will feel the need to sort the rest of the fleece and reduce it down to smaller piles of uniform fibers. Sometimes the tips of the fibers are matted or burnt from the sun—such tips can be cut off, combed open, or pulled apart. As you work with the fleece and break it down into manageable sections, shake it occasionally to allow the dirt and vegetable matter to fall out. Spread the locks apart and generally open the fleece up.

Some spinners will tease the wool at this point and begin spinning; others like to wash it without soap to remove the dirt while keeping the grease. Others, especially if the fibers are to be dyed before spinning, choose to scour the fibers, which means washing them thoroughly in soap.

There are many different "recipes" for washing and scouring fleece, and one is not necessarily more correct than another. The amount of dirt and grease in the fleece will determine how it is to be washed, and the hardness or softness of the water will affect the process and its result. Some spinners swear by detergents; others will only use nondetergent soaps. One fleece can be abused from start to finish and look beautiful; another will mat with the slightest bit of water agitation.

Here are some do's and don'ts: begin, whether washing or scouring, by soaking greasy wool in a plain water bath. Fill up a large dish pan or tub with tepid water, and gently submerge the fleece. When the water turns dark—very soon after immersion of the fibers—gently remove the fleece, dump the water, preferably in the garden, and repeat the process. Do not crowd the fibers in the pan, and never run water directly on to them. Let the fibers soak overnight in clean water to allow the water to penetrate and loosen the fibers. Remember that wool is weak and in its most vulnerable stage when wet. A sudden temperature change or shock will damage the fibers. Temperature changes must be gradual, and the fibers should not be agitated. The fleece has a natural cleaning agent of its own, and it is amazing how much dirt and grease come out during the soaking and washing process.

The spinners who prefer to keep the grease in the wool for spinning will soak and rinse the fleece in warm to hot water baths without the addition of soap after the overnight soaking. Soapless soakings preserve the natural water-repellent quality that the wool fibers have when they are on the animal. It is also possible to use a small amount of nondetergent soap and still retain a good part of the oil, especially if the fleece has a high grease content.

Wool can be scoured before or after spinning. To scour after the overnight soak, you must wash the fibers in warm to hot water with soap, in successive rinses. After

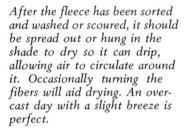

After the fleece has been sorted and washed or scoured, it should be spread out or hung in the shade to dry so it can drip, allowing air to circulate around it. Occasionally turning the fibers will aid drying. An overcast day with a slight breeze is perfect.

Bag with overspun wool fringe of gray New Zealand fleece by Candace Crockett.

An African spinning factory on Lesotho. The spinners are working mohair on Norwegian wheels. (Photograph by Dick Wezelman.)

Fumiko Pentler reeling silk from cocoons on to an old Japanese silk reeler. The cocoons are kept in warm water to loosen the gum. The filaments from at least five cocoons are reeled off together to form a heavier, stronger thread.

A Peruvian woman spinning the hair from her two alpacas. (Photograph by Skip Wollenberg.)

Woman spinning cotton in Santiago Atitlan, Guatemala. She uses a small, light spindle which rests on the ground. (Photograph by Dick Wezelman.)

(Above) A double-woven pocket hanging with a knotted pile formed of handspun, natural dyed wool. The piece, which is 8 feet wide, was woven by Candace Crockett.

Gloves—knitted of plied, handspun, natural dyed yarn—by Helen Pope.

In Memoriam *by Dina Barzel.*
30 x 12".

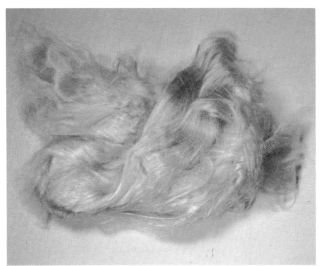

Different kinds of spinning material. Top left, mohair, which comes from the Angora goat and has a softness and sheen that makes it highly desirable for fabrics. There are both lightly washed, natural locks and washed and carded fibers shown here. Top right, Karakul fleece. Long, coarse, and hairlike, it is frequently used to spin heavy, coarse yarns for rugs and wall hangings. Bottom left, silk. Silk that cannot be reeled is sold as silk waste for spinning. Bottom right, unwashed locks from a Spelsau fleece. They are so beautiful that it seems a shame to spin them. Spelsau sheep are a Norwegian breed that produces a two-part fleece—long, hairlike fibers form an outer coating, and short, soft fibers make up an inner coating.

(Above) Anne Blinks with Flat, a mixed black Corriedale and Lincoln sheep bred to give a heavy, open fleece with some luster.

(Top and bottom left) Gloria Adamson's flock of black and white sheep in Northern California—they were especially bred to produce quality fleece for handspinning. Many spinners feel that a natural, dark fleece and carefully controlled handspinning go together. Their search for knowledge and the proper fibers has led many of them into sheep breeding on a small scale.

Guard
by Dina Barzel.
14 x 8 feet
Woven sculpture
of handspun yarns
in natural shades.

washing, the wool should be hung in the shade to drip and dry. Skeins of spun wool should be weighted to set and distribute the twist (see Chapter 2).

The natural oil protects and waterproofs the yarn, but oil will also prevent dye from penetrating the fiber. Thus fleece must be thoroughly scoured at some point for even dyeing.

Some spinners include eucalyptus oil, water softener, salt, kerosene, or lemon juice in the final scouring rinses to improve the feel of the wool. Scoured fibers are more brittle than unscoured ones, and, for successful carding and spinning, oil, in some form or another, must be added. Most spinners prefer to leave some of the natural oil to facilitate fiber preparation and spinning.

Many people who raise sheep for quality fleece have special formulas for dealing with their particular breed. Virginia Rowell, who raises Cheviot sheep in northern California, near Sacramento, has the following set of instructions for dealing with her fleece, 100% Cheviot fleece; medium grade—48s to 56s. The grease content will be less than 35%. Unless you intend to dye this fleece "in the wool," you must scour it to remove all grease. For best results, *do not scour before spinning.* Suggested washing instructions: dissolve 2 tablespoons of Calgon Water Conditioner in 5 gallons of water hot to your hand. Place ¼ pound of prepared fleece in a mesh lingerie bag or on a large square of nylon net. Gently submerse the fleece in the conditioned water, and allow it to remain *undisturbed until the water is cool.* Remove, squeeze out excess water, and then rinse once in tepid water. The fleece can be left in the bag and dried for a few seconds in a washing machine with a centrifugal action dry cycle. Take the fleece

This illustration shows the washing of fleece in eighteenth-century France. The industrial revolution brought tremendous changes, but until then the process was similar to what a handspinner would do today. The shearing barn is in the background. The fleece is washed in a large tub of water containing three parts water and one part urine. The urine cuts the grease and dissolves the encrusted perspiration salts. After washing, the fibers are rinsed in the river and hung on a rack in small bunches to air-dry. (A Diderot Pictorial Encyclopedia of Trades and Industry.)

After washing, the clean, dry fleece is picked and sorted according to length and quality. A slotted table is used so the excess bits and pieces fall through to the floor. (A Diderot Pictorial Encyclopedia of Trades and Industry.)

out of the bag and place it on a bath towel. Shake it lightly and gently, and pull apart the tips and cut ends—this procedure prevents matting of the ends. Fluff and turn the wool as it dries. The fleece is now ready to prepare for spinning.

Anne Blinks has a general formula for handling and scouring fleece that involves the use of the washing machine (without agitation). Begin by laying the whole fleece out flat and taking a good look. If you have a slotted table that the dirt and second cuts will fall through, so much the better. Take away the belly, any dung and matted bits around the hind end, any badly urine stained bits, and the lower legs. A "well skirted" fleece from New Zealand or England will probably come with all this done. One from a United States farm probably won't unless it is a show fleece. If you want to thoroughly clean the whole fleece, you will have to wash it a couple of pounds at a time, tease it lot by lot, blend, and card. If you have more than enough fleece, you can and should sort for fineness. Hairy legs to one side, neck and shoulders to the other, back either by itself or with the sides depending on how it looks. If the fleece is colored, sort it for color. A rusty look is probably from sunburn but is a nice color none the less. A good gray may give you three or four tones. If your two or three gray groups are too close together, you can get more contrast by blending one of them with white or black after the first carding. For example, you could card a batt of gray and a batt of white (or black) together.

Now for the wash. Take as much fleece as you need for the immediate future. Pick it open and discard all the dirt, weed seeds, second cuts, and stained bits that you can at this stage. Put the picked-over wool in a good-sized can (a clean plastic garbage can is fine), and cover with water from the hose. Let it stand overnight at least—24 hours is better. Next dump it out on the lawn. If you can make a frame of 2 x 4's with ¼" hardware cloth stretched over it on which to dump and drain it, that is fine—but the grass will do. Lift the soggy wool carefully, and put it in the empty basket of a top-loading, spin-type washing machine, and spin the water out.

From this point on, one bucket full of damp wool is enough to handle at once. Remove the wet wool and put it back into the bucket. Wipe or rinse the mud from the inside of the tub. Fill with *hot* water. Add about ½ cup of Tide and dissolve. How much soap to use depends on how dirty your fleece is and how delicate. Every fleece can be different. Add the wool, push it under, and *leave it alone* until the water is lukewarm. Do not agitate at any time. After some practice, you will be able to feel if the wool is clean. Too much soap and soak will kill the luster; too little leaves it gray or yellow. It is better to do two washes than one that is too strong.

Now spill out this dirty, soapy water. Then remove the wool carefully, wipe and rinse the tub, and refill with lukewarm water. You may need to repeat the wash with the lukewarm water and less soap than the first time. If not, add ¼ cup Downy or some other fabric softener (but not a pink one). Add the wet wool, push it under the water, and open it out under the water gently. Spill out this water, lift out the wool, wipe the machine, repeat with a second rinse. Now the wool can be put on the wire frame again or on a sheet or table to dry in the shade. Open it out from time to time as it drys but do not tease it at this stage. Repeat all this with any remaining buckets of wool.

All the wool will probably need a light spray of oil and water and a rest in a plastic bag before being teased, carded, and spun. Olive, mineral, neats foot and kerosene, and commercial oil will all work, but do not oil more wool than you expect to spin within a couple of weeks at most.

CARBONIZING

There is an almost universal cheer and joyfulness among spinning workers with their to-be-spun fleeces. Such levity of spirit, however suspect is philosophers, is common in the literature as well as in the activities of the wool worker. This little poem, with an introduc-

tion from *Scottish Woolens* tells lightheartedly of the results of carbonizing, a process by which burrs and other vegetable matter are removed from wool.

A young man regretted to the great Dr. Johnson that his attempts to become a philosopher had all ended in failure because cheerfulness would break through. The late Mr. Monbert also found that even in the Wool Trade cheerfulness would break through, so we end on a somewhat frivolous note by quoting lesson VII of his *The Wool Trade: A Guide for Beginners*. Those who wish to continue the course will find the complete set in *Rhymes of the Wool Market*.

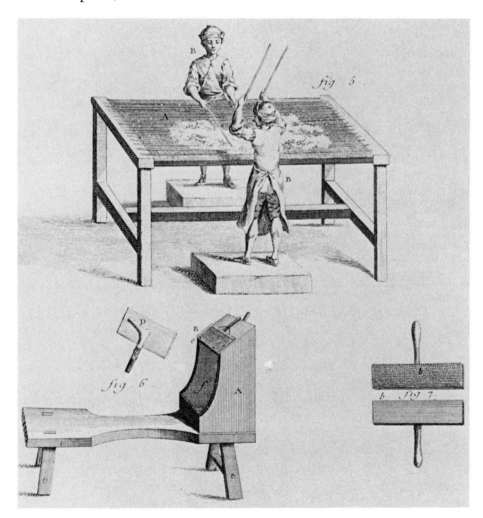

*After picking and sorting, the fibers are beaten to rid them of any vegetable matter or dirt that might remain. The beating also fluffs and separates the fibers. After this, the fibers are arranged in parallel order by carding with a pair of hand carders. (*A Diderot Pictorial Encyclopedia of Trades and Industry.*)*

Carbonizing is a commercial process done after scouring that involves passing the wool through a weak solution of sulfuric acid. The wool is slowly dried, and the acid, which does not evaporate, concentrates in the vegetable matter. Then the wool is crushed or beaten to reduce the vegetable matter to dust, which is drawn out by suction fans, after which the wool fibers are neutralized and rinsed.

Carbonizing is only one of the mechanical and chemical steps industry puts wool through in order to arrive at a thoroughly standard uniform product.

A Burr is quite a common seed
That looks just like a centipede,
When, in the combing, it uncoils
And spreads itself among your noils.
When you observe them first, no doubt
You do your best to pick them out;
But in the end you'll find it wiser
To send them to the carboniser.
For, if they're woven in a shirt,
Men scratch themselves until they hurt;
And if girls get them in their undies
They musn't go to Church on Sundays,
For, when they're kneeling down in prayer
They shouldn't scratch themselves and swear.

STORING WOOL

Wool fleece should be stored in a dark, cool place, safe from moth infestation. Direct sunlight will dry out the fibers and literally bake them. Wool retains moisture and is best not stored in plastic bags. Fleece wrapped in brown paper or newspaper—sealed carefully—or stored in large paper grocery bags is protected from light and is able to breath.

A greasy fleece should not be stored too long before washing, since eventually the grease dries up and the fibers become heavy and lifeless. Mothballs can be used to discourage moths, but, if infestation does occur, it can be stopped by freezing the wool for a few days.

I have one friend who uses great quantities of raw fleece for spinning up heavy, textured wool yarns. She often freezes her fleece as an anti-moth tactic, and has been heard to report that, although she has lost her ice cream, she has never lost a fleece.

MOHAIR

Mohair is the long, silky, snow white fleece of the Angora goat. The fibers cascade from the animal in gentle curves and waves. The goat is indigenous to Asiatic Turkey and takes its name from the early trade that flourished around the city of Angora. During the early part of the nineteenth century, when the demand for mohair increased sharply, Angora goats were shipped to all parts of the world. Today there are many herds in South Africa and in the western part of the United States, particularly in Texas. In adapting them to new climates, the Angora goat is frequently crossed with ordinary goats, but the fleece of the progeny is shorter, coarser, and less lustrous.

The physical structure of the mohair fiber is similar to that of wool, but, as with other hair fibers, the scales are only indicated and not developed. This surface smoothness makes the fibers lustrous and slippery. The age and sex of the animal, as well as its breeding, determine the fineness of the fleece. There are many grades and varieties, with the finest coming from the youngest animals. The goats are usually sheared once a year, and the fibers frequently reach a length of from 10 to 12".

Mohair is a durable fiber, dyes easily, and retains its beautiful silklike luster. Mohair yarns are frequently brushed to raise the fiber ends. This brushing gives a soft, furry surface. Because of its slipperiness, especially when mechanically carded and combed, mohair is difficult for the beginning spinner to handle. The very fine first shearings from the young full-blooded animals are difficult even for the experienced spinner.

CASHMERE

Cashmere, described as the wool "nearest to heaven," is another goat fiber. It comes from the fleece of the Cashmere goat, a small, short-legged, frugal animal that inhabits the barren high plateaus of Asia. The finest cashmere comes from China, Mongolia, Manchuria, and Tibet (in that order). The higher the altitude, the finer the fleece. This goat, like many hair-bearing animals in cold climates, has a double fleece. The soft, fine fibers, which are highly prized, are close to the body underneath the coarse outer guard hairs. These short, down fibers are combed or plucked by the nomadic herdsmen who tend the animals. A single goat produces about as much usable fiber as an Angora rabbit—only a few ounces every year. The natural color of the cashmere down is a pale warm gray or a natural brown.

Cashmere fibers follow the ancient silk road and come down from the high regions in small bundles. The quantity varies from year to year, depending on price and the political situation. Cashmere is an expensive fiber, usually available only in small quantities that typically come in once each year.

Because of their fineness and density, cashmere yarns have a luxurious softness. The soft down fibers are clean, and, although short, are easy to spin. The guard hairs, which are long and coarse and which spin into bristly, highly textured yarn, are also available to

The Angora goat has long silky locks that cascade to the ground. The lustrous white fleece is called mohair.

The Cashmere goat is found in the high plateaus and mountains of Asia. Its soft downy under coat is combed and plucked for the cashmere wool trade.

157

the handspinner. The difference between the downy softness of the under hairs and the bristly roughness of the outer guard hairs makes it hard to believe that they come from the same animal.

Like wool, cashmere has felting properties. In China, the down was traditionally felted into hats used as protection from the cold winds on the high plateaus. The hats, as with many woven cashmere fabrics, were brushed to form a beautiful, soft, ripply surface.

CAMEL HAIR

The two-humped Bactrian camel grows a thick winter undercoat, which it sheds naturally in thin, downy sheets. Like the Cashmere goat, the camel produces two coats: a soft, warm inner down and a rough, hairy outer layer. The term "camel's hair" usually refers to the light brown inner fibers, which have good strength and durability, and spin easily into a soft, light brown yarn. The outer guard hairs are sometimes available and spin into a coarse yarn. They are frequently mixed with straw and are difficult and time-consuming to pick clean.

The camel is primarily a beast of burden, and, as it travels the trade routes through northern Africa, Central Asia, and Mongolia, there is always somebody bringing up the rear, whose job entails picking up the fibers as they fall off. Camels shed all year round, and each animal produces from 30 to 40 pounds of fiber a year.

WOOL FROM THE LLAMA, ALPACA, AND VICUNA

The llama, alpaca, and vicuña are all humpless members of the camel family living primarily on the *altiplano* of Peru, Bolivia, and Argentina. Although attempts have been made and continue to be

(Above) The two-humped Bactrian camel sheds its warm undercoat in hunks. The fibers spin into soft brown yarns with exceptional insulating qualities.

The llama is a South American member of the camel family. It was domesticated as a beast of burden, and the fibers have been used in making textiles for centuries.

made, these animals have not been bred elsewhere with any success. They all have similar physical characteristics, but differ in size.

The llama (a wild form is called the guanaco) is a domesticated beast of burden that produces a long, dense, fine wool. The alpaca is smaller than the llama, with much longer and finer wool. It has been selectively bred for wool quality for centuries. The fleece of the alpaca is lustrous and silky, and the fiber has good elasticity and durability. When sheared regularly, it averages a yearly growth of from 6 to 8". If not clipped, it can grow up to a length of 30". The animal, which reaches a height of about 4 feet, is not easily domesticated. The fibers, because of their length and softness and beautiful range of natural colors, have been highly prized by handspinners for many, many generations. Alpaca fibers can be found in browns, red browns, grays, blacks, and whites. These fibers are carefully sorted according to quality and color and are exported in the form of scoured, combed top. Yarns spun from the alpaca are soft, fine, dense, and very warm. Like mohair fabrics, textiles made from alpaca are frequently brushed to raise the nap.

The fleece from the llama is inferior to that of the alpaca and is not as readily available. There is usually a great deal of color variation within a single llama fleece. Alpaca and llama fibers do not have developed scales, and, as a result, the yarns produced do not have the airy, bouncy quality of wool.

The vicuña, which is found in the high Andean uplands in altitudes of 10,000 to 13,000 feet, has never been successfully domesticated. The wool, meat, and skin of this small, delicate animal are all highly valued. It is commonly held that the vicuña produces the finest wool in existence. The fibers measure 25,000 to the inch, about half the thickness of the finest sheep's wool. A single fleece weighs about a pound. At the time of the Inca empire, the wool from the vicuña was reversed for royalty. Today, the shy, timid animal, which is easily trapped and killed, is nearly extinct. It is hoped that new protective laws will increase their numbers, and perhaps, in the future, the fibers will be available to more handspinners.

QIVIUT

These fibers come from the musk oxen, which is found today in the uninhabited regions of Arctic North America and Greenland. The musk oxen is a prehistoric-looking animal with heavy, droopy, curved horns. The animal has recently been domesticated for its wool in an attempt to augment the arctic economy. The animal is covered with dark brown, coarse guard hairs, so long that they sometimes reach the ground; these fibers bear the brunt of the rain and snow. Underneath this shaggy mantle is an inner down coat of fine, soft, light brown hairs, which insulate the animal from the intense cold. In the spring, the inner coat

Esther McKinley tells of an experience spinning the fur of the chinchilla. She wanted to thoroughly blend the fibers to produce an even yarn, but found the fine fibers to be like down feathers and impossible to handle. Her solution was to make a silk bag for the vacuum cleaner and tease the fibers so they were sucked into the vacuum and stored in the silk bag.

breaks away and works its way through the guard hairs to literally peel from the animal in sheets. The fine, soft hairs are called by the Eskimo name of qiviut. The down is similar to cashmere, but the fibers are longer. Fine yarns spun from qiviut are incredibly light, soft, and warm. Presently, the fibers are machine spun and knitted into specialty items by the Eskimo women. The animals are still very rare, but small quantities of the fibers occasionally find their way into spinning outlets. The price is very high, but a little bit of this exotic fiber goes a long way.

DOG HAIRS

In the past, the undercoats of dogs have frequently been used—especially in combination with wool—to produce soft, textured yarns. Many spinners are interested in dog hairs because they are readily available and usually free. Not everyone is in a position to have a sheep or Angora goat, but a dog is fairly easy to come by and it seems only natural that the combings, which are usually thrown away, should be spun into usable yarns. Fibers are where you find them, and dog hairs long enough for spinning can be an important fiber source.

Only certain breeds produce a proper coat for spinning. Generally speaking, these are dogs bred for cold climates. The most popular is the samoyed, whose hair spins into a yarn very much like that of the Angora rabbit, very soft and white, with a brushed, woolly look. Sometimes the short, harsh fibers of terrier type dogs are mixed with wool—the dog hairs give texture and the wool gives strength and cohesiveness. Dog hair has a tendency to be very "fly away," and, when spun, tends also to be some-

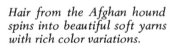

Hair from the Afghan hound spins into beautiful soft yarns with rich color variations.

what lifeless and weak. Blending it with wool makes for easier spinning and a more buoyant, useful yarn. Long fibers are the easiest to clean and deal with, and unmatted brushings and combings are preferred to cut hairs. The hair from the afghan hound, because of the length and gradations in color, makes an especially beautiful yarn. Unfortunately, the hair from some dogs has a very strong odor when moist.

HAIR FROM THE ANGORA RABBIT

Fibers from the Angora rabbit are soft and silky and used for spinning soft, fuzzy yarns that are especially beautiful when brushed. The fibers are difficult to handle, and the spun yarn is not particularly durable. The Angora rabbit is difficult to raise and gives only a small amount of fiber. The hairs, about 5" in length, are usually plucked or combed and only rarely cut. The animal moults frequently and the fibers are collected at this time. The best quality comes from the young adults—as the rabbits age, the fibers become coarser and more hairlike.

HORSE HAIR AND GOAT HAIR

Hair from the tails of horses is also available to the handspinner. Like most goat hair, it is coarse, bristly, and not very flexible. Both horse hair and goat hair are difficult to spin and generally require the addition of oil for spinning cohesiveness. These fibers can be mixed with wool for special effects and are usually used that way.

CONCLUSION

Whether spinning the rare fibers of the vicuña, the combings from neighborhood dogs, or wool from local sheep, animals offer a constantly replenished wealth of fibers

that never cease to amaze and delight. Spinning offers the opportunity to experience live fibers and, perhaps for the first time, to understand what such age-old fibers as cashmere, mohair, and merino are all about. The opportunity to see the sheep in the field, to take the fleece home, to feel and handle, to select and watch the fibers as they go from field to yarn, is a rare and rewarding experience.

We are fortunate in that we have access to the fibers of the world. We can spin fibers from the Peruvian *altiplano* or those from the goats living on high mountain peaks of Mongolia.

The machines may make perfect yarns, but they deny one the understanding and experience. Spinners of the past were forced to spin of necessity. We are fortunate—we can experience the pleasure without the pain.

Various animal fibers. On the right are the long silky locks of a Mohair goat; on the left bottom is hair from an Angora rabbit; and, on top, the soft down of a musk ox.

CHAPTER EIGHT

Vegetable Fibers

Egyptians say it was Isis who invented and taught them the art of spinning, the Chinese believe they were taught by the consort of their Emperor Yao, almost all nations ascribe the honor to the ingenuity of the fair sex. Lydians to Arachne, Greeks to Minerva, Peruvians to Mamacella, wife to Manco-capac, their first sovereign.

Spinning Machinery
by Andrew Gray Edinburgh, 1819.
Printed for Archibald
Constable and Company

The cotton seed is planted in the spring, and about two months later flower buds appear. They take about three weeks to open and gradually change in color from white to yellow to pink to dark red. Then they fall off, leaving the pods, which are called bolls. Each boll contains many seeds covered with hairs. As the boll ripens, the fibers attached to the seeds expand and eventually split the boll open, exposing the white fluffy mass of cotton.

Vegetable fibers come from plants: from the seeds as hairs, as with cotton; from the bast (or inner core) of stems of plants like flax or hemp; from the leaves, as with sisal; and from outer protective coatings, such as bark and husks, of fibers from trees like the coconut tree. The quality of the fiber depends on many things: species, seed, soil, method of cultivation, climatic conditions, and time of harvesting.

The vegetable fibers discussed in this chapter are the traditional, readily available fibers specifically cultivated and developed for spinning. However, it is important to keep in mind that many very usable fibers are not commonly used as a result of high labor costs or limited availability, or because something else is a little cheaper to produce or a little better for commercial purposes.

Your natural, immediate environment is probably full of plants that in one way or another might be used as sources for fiber. Wild plant fibers of various types are frequently used by people who live in places where a relatively simple technology prevals. Studying the textiles of such cultures can provide insight into many unused fibers and simple methods of preparing them. In the past, plants from the nettle family provided many American Indians with a usable fiber for very fine textiles. Corn husks and cedar bark were also used with great sophistication. The inner bark of some trees has been cut into strips, boiled in lye, dried, and then shredded or beaten into soft fibers or—if still coarse—twisted into strong ropes. Many varieties of grass, straw, and reed can also be twisted and plied, not necessarily into gold—as with the miller's daughter in the fairy tale *Rumplestiltskin*—but certainly into usable cords.

Fiber plants grow widely and are there for the finding. Any climbing

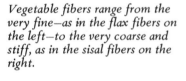

Vegetable fibers range from the very fine—as in the flax fibers on the left—to the very coarse and stiff, as in the sisal fibers on the right.

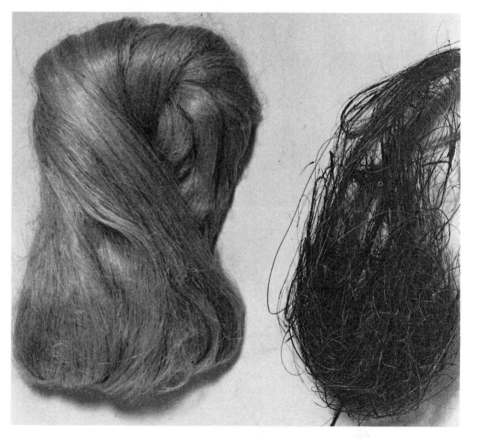

plant with a flexible stem is a likely suspect. When seeking fibers to spin, look for long, stringy stems; tall, fast-growing annuals with straight stems; trees with easily removed bark; and plants with large, tough leaves. Chances are that under the surface are spinnable fibers that can be obtained by scraping, beating, or rotting. This study of some of the plants that have been widely used and specifically cultivated for use as fibers, and this brief examination of methods developed for extracting such fibers, is meant to give insight into the nature of all vegetable fibers.

GENERAL CHARACTERISTICS

Plant fibers are composed primarily of cellulose, which usually exists in combination with waxy matter, coloring matters, tannins, and pectin matter. Vegetable fibers can be destroyed by strong acids, and, when exposed to direct flame, they burn quickly and smell like burning leaves. In general, yarns spun from cellulose fibers lack loft and airiness. They spin into dense, compact yarns with little elasticity. If the fibers are spun dry, the yarns will be uneven and hairy. If the fibers are wet spun—moistened by wetting the fingers during spinning or the fibers just prior to spinning—smooth, controlled yarns can be produced.

Cellulose fibers have consistently good moisture absorbency and can withstand high temperatures. They are more flammable than animal fibers, but, although they will mildew, they will not be attacked by moths. On the whole, vegetable fibers are coarser, harder, and less lustrous than animal fibers. They do not have the natural oils of wool fibers and therefore are frequently spun with the addition of oil or water to make them more pliable and cohesive. Unlike wool fibers, vegetable fibers are stronger when wet. Cotton and flax are by far the most spinnable of the plant fibers because of fineness, natural twist, and surface roughness. Hemp and jute are coarse and resistant in comparison, but seem flexible and fine when compared to the leaf fibers, such as sisal.

Many plant fibers come in long lengths, which are tricky for hand-spinning, because they have a tendency to tangle and not draft. They can be cut into shorter lengths, and often are cut in the mills, but such shortening results in a weaker yarn with a more abrasive surface. Special methods for dealing with vegetable fibers are discussed and illustrated below:

COTTON

Cotton, *gossypium hirsutum*, is a seed hair. It is a short fiber with good cohesive qualities. Because of the cohesive quality, the fibers are easy to spin, but the short lengths make cotton difficult for the beginning spinner to deal with. Spinning a smooth, evenly twisted cotton thread takes practice.

Although cotton was used in early Mexico and Peru, India is thought of as the center of cotton industry from 1500 B.C. to 1500 A.D. Over the centuries, a great deal of experimental work has been done with cotton, resulting in hundreds of different varieties and strains. Modern cotton plants produce an improved fiber and have been bred to flourish in a variety of climates.

By 1500 A.D., cotton was known throughout the world. It is traditionally thought of as the fiber that clothed the masses, probably because it grows best in hot, humid climates where many poor people live. It was not used much in Europe or colonial America until after the coming of the Industrial Revolution. The trouble with spinning cotton had always been the difficulty of removing the fibers from the seeds. All of the seeds had to be removed before the fibers were usable, and this removal involved much tedious hand labor. The cotton grown in America is different from the cotton grown in India—the American fibers are more firmly attached to the seeds. So even with very cheap labor, obtaining the fiber was time consuming and uneconomical. However, in 1793, Eli Whitney invented the cotton gin (gin is short for engine), which mechanically separated the hairs from the seeds. The Industrial Revolution that followed can be said to be the story of developing machines to handle cotton. In any case, as the machines took over, cotton became the cheap and superior fiber. It remained the world's most widely used fiber until the invention and cheap manufacture of synthetic fibers in the mid-twentieth century.

THE PLANT

The cotton plant, reaching a height of from 4 to 6 feet requires a warm, humid climate and moist, sandy soil. All these conditions play a part in determining the quality of the fiber. Cotton is indigenous to all warm climates, but is commercially grown in only a few.

The cotton fiber begins as a hollow tube emerging from a cell in the seed wall. The tube fills with protoplasm and grows in length. Then gradually, in layers, the sugars of the protoplasm are transferred into many layers of cellulose, which build up spirally on the inside of the tube, giving the ultimate fiber strength and flexibility. After the boll—the rounded seed pod—opens, each fiber dries into a flat, twisted, ribbonlike shape with a rough

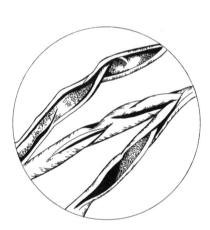

The twisting of the cotton fiber can only be seen with magnification. As the fiber matures, it dries into a flat, twisted, ribbon-like shape with little or no luster. The central canal of the fiber cell, the lumen, collapses and spirals, causing the fiber to twist in different directions. This twist facilitates spinning.

surface and a collapsed inner canal. This inner canal allows the fiber to absorb moisture, and the twists give the fiber cohesiveness, allowing the fibers to kink together and interlock during spinning. Even so, cotton is much less elastic than wool or silk. Spinning, however, depends not only on the nature and amount of twist, but on the length and fineness of the fiber. Also, the cotton fiber has a waxlike outer coating, which aids in spinning.

Cotton fabrics, because of their rough surface and the many ends of

The production and manufacture of cotton was not taken up by the North American growers until 1770—three years after the invention of the spinning jenny by Hargreaves. Before that it was more expensive than flax and considered a luxury. It was called by the East Indian name of "hum'hum."

the short fibers, catch dust and stains and so soil quickly; but they also wash easily and can withstand the effects of hot water and rough treatment. Cotton fibers are not damaged by strong soaps or by boiling water. In its natural state, the fiber does not dye easily. In industrial use, spun yarns and cotton fabrics are frequently treated with a strong solution of caustic soda or lye in a process called mercerizing. This treatment actually changes the fiber structure so it becomes heavier, stronger, and more readily susceptible to dyes. If the caustic soda is applied while the fibers are under tension, the structural change imparts a luster.

Because of the problem in dyeing cotton, many spinners are interested in using natural brown cotton. Brown cotton has been largely ignored by commercial cotton growers and is therefore rare and very difficult to come by. As it now exists, it is an inferior grade of cotton with a staple length of less than ¾"—but with a beautiful shade of brown. The plant itself is relatively unproductive and is known by several names. Seeds are sometimes available from spinning suppliers. Brown-fibered types of cotton arise in all varieties of cotton as mutations, but they are rigorously eliminated in order to prevent any influence on the white crop. The Acadians in Louisiana have a long history of growing small patches of brown cotton for their own use in domestic handmade textiles. This cotton was traditionally brought to be ginned on the last day of ginning after all the white cotton had been run through.

Although the varieties and strains are infinite, there are three basic kinds of cotton available. The most desirable and the easiest to spin has long, fine fibers varying in length from 1 to 1½". This group includes the Egyptian, Peruvian, and Sea Island types. The second group, usually referred to as American Uplands, is coarser and shorter, varying in length from ½ to 1½". The third group of fibers, "Old World Types," are coarse and dull and vary from 3/8 to 1" in length.

PREPARING COTTON FIBERS FOR SPINNING

If you collect cotton from the field, the first step is to separate the fluffy mass of soft hairs from the hard burst boll and other miscellaneous debris. Each boll contains many seeds, and each seed is totally covered with short, soft hairs. The hairs must be plucked from each seed. To do this, fan the fibers out from the seed, and work around the seed, plucking deftly as you go. Seeds can be worked out of some strains of cotton by taking an iron rod or smooth, hard stick and rolling forward on a flat board or stone. After removing the seeds, the fibers can be teased or fluffed and massed into loose pads, sometimes called laps, and spun directly. Cotton fibers can be further prepared by carding. Cotton carders are similar to wool carders, but the

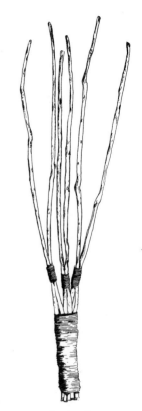

A pre-Spanish Southwest American tool used for whipping cotton. After plucking the fibers from the seeds, some spinners whipped them with long, thin sticks to tease and blend the fibers. Any flexible stick can be used. It is a tedious task, usually done on a padded surface. This method for treating cotton is found in many cultures with simple technologies.

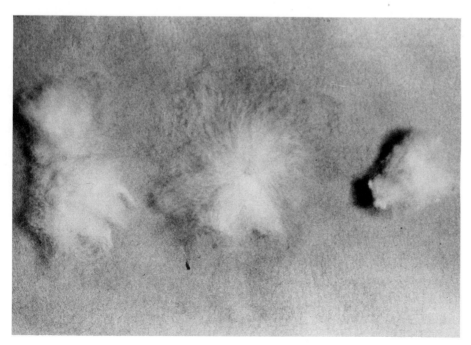

A single cotton seed surrounded by the seed hairs is shown at right, followed by the hairs fanned for plucking and the plucked fibers.

Fine cotton thread can be spun on a light, delicate spindle with a clay head for a whorl. This is a pre-Columbian spindle used for spinning cotton.

teeth are more finely set for the shorter, finer fibers. Any carders can be used, and only a light quick carding is necessary.

In many parts of the world where cotton is spun by hand, it is beaten with a flexible switch to fluff and loosen the fibers. Sometimes a bow is made by stretching a cord between the ends of a flexible rod, and the cord is twanged over the cotton. The vibration fluffs the cotton up. Many spinners like to take these fluffed up or carded laps, and form them into "punis." A puni is somewhat like a wool rolag and is especially nice for wheel spinning. To make a puni, wrap the cotton fibers tightly around a smooth dowel or stick (see illustration on page 168). Slip the rolled fibers off the stick, and spin from the puni end.

Commercially picked cotton is immediately ginned and tightly compacted into large bales weighing hundreds of pounds. Small amounts, however, are available from most spinning suppliers. The fibers come wadded together in a generally unappealing mass, though good quality cotton is sometimes available in sliver form. One method of preparing ginned or handplucked cotton for spinning is to steam the fibers. To do this, suspend the fibers over boiling water in such a way that steam will penetrate the entire mass. A colander or sieve placed in a large pan with a few inches of water in the bottom works well. Cover with a lid, and steam the cotton for a few minutes just prior to spinning. The moist, expanded fibers will spin into a smooth, even yarn.

Cotton is highly flammable, and should be treated with care when near flame or steam. One of the early objections to cotton was—when compared to wool—its relatively high tendency to burst into flames when exposed to heat. Working with cotton, especially when steaming, can be dangerous and should be done with care.

SPINNING COTTON

The primary consideration in spinning cotton centers on the length of the fibers. The drawing distance must be very short, with the hands close together and working rhythmically. Wet your fingers and run them up and down the yarn as the twist runs up to even the yarn and tuck in the ends. When cotton is spun on the hand spindle, the

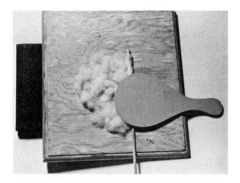

Whipped cotton or cotton carded on hand cards can be formed into tight rolags that are perfect for spinning. Use a dowel, a board, and a paddle (a paddle from the toy store minus the rubber band and ball). Slant the board on the far end, put the prepared cotton down, and place the dowel at the end nearest the body. Roll up and around, always in the same direction, with the paddle. Rub only one way so the cotton is compressed tightly around the stick. To begin, push down hard on the stick and hold the paddle gently. After the cotton is rolled on to the stick, roll more in the same direction by pushing down hard on the paddle to compact the fibers.

bottom tip of the spindle is frequently rested on something solid so the full weight of the spindle is not spun on the short fibers. This stops the spindle from crashing to the floor and gives the fingers a delicate control. Try to keep the fibers fanned so they form a triangle as they feed into the twist.

Spinning cotton on the wheel is mainly a matter of adjusting the treadling and take-in on the bobbin to the short length of the fibers. The yarn must be well twisted before it winds on to the bobbin or it will pull apart. During spinning, the drafting area—whether you are using the short draw or the long—should not be too close to the orifice. Working too close to the spinning wheel orifice with the short fibers will create weak spots because the twist will not have a chance to even out, so be sure to keep the drafting area back from the orifice.

FLAX

Flax is a bast fiber derived from the inner stalk of the flax plant (*linum usitatissimum*). Although the words flax and linen are frequently used interchangeably, flax refers specifically to the fiber, and linen to the goods made of flax.

Flax has a long and fascinating tradition. Its fibers have been spun and woven into linen since prehistoric times, and, until the end of the eighteenth centu*ry* with the advent of machines for dealing with cotton, flax was the most important vegetable fiber used for textiles in Europe and colonial America. Flax is an easy crop to raise, and, for many settlers on this continent, it was the single textile crop that could be grown as soon as a plot of land was cleared. It is interesting to note that flax has always been associ-

A Cuna Indian from the San Blas Islands off the west coast of Panama, shown spinning cotton on a long spindle. The bottom tip of the spindle rests on the ground—this prevents the weight of the spindle from pulling too hard on the short fibers.

169

ated with cleanliness, and, in some religions, clean white linen is regarded as a symbol of divine purity.

The flax fiber, like other bast fibers, must be separated from the stalk of the flax plant through a long process that involves rotting the outside layer, breaking up the fibers, and separating the long "line" fibers from the short "tow" fibers. The long, tedious process involved considerable hand labor. Complete mechanization has not been achieved, and flax today is cultivated commercially primarily where there is cheap labor. In the past, the processing of flax was primarily a domestic occupation, closely bound up with the agrarian life of a preindustrial era. Cultivation spread throughout Europe in the Middle Ages, and, at that time, flax spinning was a common occupation of all women regardless of class.

The processing of the fiber is basically the same for all bast fibers (flax, hemp, jute). The production techniques of flax can give the modern fiber worker some understanding of methods used in preindustrial times and places. The complicated processing of the plant took on local peculiarities and rituals, which were frequently depicted in paintings, songs, and poems. Luther compared the sufferings that mankind has to endure in life on earth with the tortures flax has to go through while being worked—flax must literally be beaten and ripped to pieces in order for the good fibers to be separated from the bad. After it is spun and woven, flax becomes soft and supple only with wear and washing. Pliny's words "Semper iniuria melious"—always improved by rough treatment—refer to the inherent nature of flax.

The working of flax remained a domestic occupation well into the twentieth century in the southeastern part of the United States. Rebecca Hyatt, in *Mary Lou's Kiverlid, A Sketch of Mountain Life*, offers a glimpse into that time of transition.

"I never hanker fer fetched-on truck to make wipin'-towels, fer hit jist nacherly don't soak up the wet as good. I bin a pesterin' Calhoun to put out a little patch thar yon side the goose-lot. Men-folks on this creek air gittin' too dilatory to work up flax anymore, dependin' on everything store-bought."

"You air right," exclaimed Nancy, "I ha'n't seed much flax worked out in a good bit. The last time I tried to scutch some hands that war raised a few yeer back hit war so bresh hit's no manner o' count. I reckon jist too old and layin' too long."

"No, hit don't git to be no 'count jist bein' growed a long time. What ailed yer flax, Nancy, hit wus jist left on the ground too long when you spread hit to rot, jist spiled that away with too much rottenin' and not fittin' to work up. Calhoun is breakin' some flax today while he's watchin' his coal pit, as wus spread hit to rot nigh six weeks back. Sowed hit the right time too. When the white oak leaves gits the size o' squirrel's yeers "hits time to start drappin' corn and sowin' flax. Calhoun's pappy," continued Granny, "allus looked after his own flax work. His rule was to sow hit on Good Friday an' pull hit the first of August, an' sow hit thick as hair on a hog's back to make the fiber long an' fine."

"Now I ha'n't never ricollected old Uncle Jessie," broke in Nancy, "but hit's bin told me

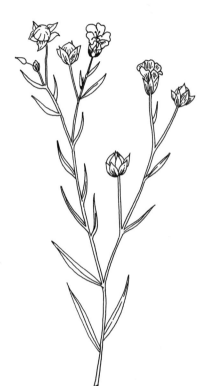

The wild flax plant of the ancient world. Over the centuries selective breeding has elongated the plant so that it flowers and branches at the top of a long stem to produce longer and finer fibers.

he was a master hand with flax."

"You've heerd right, Nancy. Hit air wasteful to handle flax keer-less. If hit ain't rotted sufficient and if you ain't keerful with yer scutchin' an' hacklin' hit wastes a sight bad. If the scutchin' ain't done complete the shives'll pull too much tow out'n the hackle in sich away that most yer flax air in the tow possums."

Shad said: "tow possums, Granny?"

"Yes," sputtered the oldest one, "ha'n't you never lurnt nothin'? Possums is the wads of coarse tow you first hackle out'n a hand o' flax. You weave hit in wagon kivers an' bed tickin' and other rough stuff. Hits best to bile the tow thread out good in a pot o' ashes to saften hit up and break the stiff out'n hit afore hits wove.

We allus gathered up the drappin's under the flax-break and 'round the scutchin' board, and 'u'd take an' spin hit into coarse thread. Then we'd git out the old rope-works an' twist hit, makin' bed cords. Stuff of any sort made out'n tow an' flax, jist last might nigh allus.

As I wus sayin', atter the tow is all hackled out, what's left is the flax fer fine weavin', men-folks Sunday-meetin' clothes, table kivers, an' bed sheets an' the like. I'm aimin' to have some sewin' thread spun out'n this flax," enthused Granny. "I bin lately most too ailin' to spin, but they warn't a woman-person miles around could beat me at hit ever since I wus a strip of a gal."

CHARACTERISTICS OF THE FLAX FIBER

Flax fibers have an irregular surface and natural twist that give the fibers cohesive qualities and make them especially spinnable. Flax is about 70% cellulose, and a single fiber consists of a number of cells held together by pectic substances. These pectic substances resist natural dyes, but the flax fiber responds well to synthetic dyes. Flax is frequently bleached to a pure white. The bleaching process removes the natural gum that coats the fibers and allows them to dye more readily. Traditionally, though, flax is left in its natural color, which varies from a pale yellowish white to gray. The particular quali-ties of the best grades of flax are luster, strength, length, and fine-ness. The fiber is a good conductor of heat, so linen garments always feel cool. The fibers are pliable, and, because of surface irregularity, have good holding qualities. Flax has little elasticity, and, conse-quently, linen fabrics wrinkle easily.

THE FLAX PLANT

The flax plant grows easily in most climates. It requires both a good quality sandy soil free of weeds and plenty of water. It does better under cloudy skies and takes about three months to reach maturity. It is an annual in temperate and cool climates, and a winter annual in warm climates. Flax is grown for fiber and for seeds, but the two crops are treated differently. Seed flax, which is widely cultivated in the United States, produces a low-grade, near useless fiber. The seeds for fiber flax are planted close to-gether so the plants will grow straight and tall with little branch-ing. The plant has three parts: the outer bark; a central woody core, which is pithy but hollow when dry; and the fiber—between the woody center and the outer bark—which runs in layers from root to blossom.

Flax grows to a height of about 40", with narrow leaves and five-

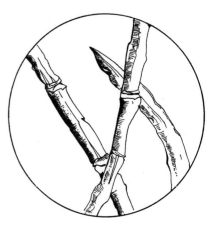

Under the microscope, the flax fiber looks rather like trans-parent bamboo. It has an irregu-lar surface, with knuckles. It is about 70% cellulose, and a single filament consists of a number of cells or parts held together by pectic substances.

Rippling. Small handfuls of the harvested flax straw are drawn through the iron teeth of a rippling comb to remove the seeds and leaves. Seeds from mature plants are saved for the next planting.

Breaking. The dried flax is drawn back and forth over a slotted opening as a heavy wooden blade is brought deftly down over and over again to loosen the fibers from the inner core. Breaking can also be done with a wooden mallet or hammer.

petaled blue flowers. One of the greatest pleasures to be had from raising flax is the view of a sweeping field of blue flax flowers. The plants are harvested before the seeds ripen, which prevents strong growth of the woody parts of the plant and insures fine fibers. The plants are pulled from the ground rather than cut—so the fibers will be as long as possible—tied into bundles, and allowed to dry for a few days. Then the seeds and leaves are removed during the process called rippling (see the illustration at left). After this, the flax is bundled up into small groups and submerged in water for rotting. This process is called retting and is ideally done in slow moving water.

As fermentation sets in, bacteria dissolve the softer cells of the bark and rot the gum that binds the fibers to the inner core. The fiber cells remain unaffected, unless retting goes too long. Both the temperature and the chemical composition of the water will affect the color of the flax. Warm, soft water accelerates fermentation, or retting, and cold water slows it down. Retting can be done in still or running water or by dew. In some parts of Europe, the stalks are saved and retting is done in the winter snows. The retting process takes two to three weeks, and, needless to say, is not pleasant, since the rotting stalks contaminate air and water. The process is complete when the fibers strip easily.

After retting, the bundles are spread out in the sun to dry, or sometimes they are placed on a rack over a low fire. As the flax dries, it becomes highly flammable. In the past, whole villages were burned as a result of flax fires. If you are doing this at a school, the kiln room (if there is one) is the perfect place for fast drying.

After drying, the brittle straw is unbundled, and lengths are pounded and beaten to loosen the fibers. A flax "break" is traditionally used for this (see the illustration on page 172). As the blade of the break is brought down on the flax stalk, the woody inner core breaks up and falls out, while the fibers only bend. What does not fall out is then beaten out with a wooden swingling, or scutching, knife. Scutching also straightens the fibers.

Then, finally, the fibers are combed to separate the short, coarse "tow" from the long, lustrous "line." This process is referred to as hetcheling, heckling, or hackling. We do the same thing when we heckle a political speaker —we try to separate the sound material from the waste. The flax hackle, usually a block of wood with several rows of projecting teeth, is clamped to a table or bench. Usually a series of hackles are used, beginning with coarse, and moving to very fine. As the fibers are drawn back and forth, over 70% of the flax is left in the teeth of the hackle and on the floor as tow, to be gathered and spun into short fibered yarns. The long line that is left in the hands is twisted into hanks and eventually spun into a fine, very strong, lustrous linen.

SPINNING FLAX

Flax, like other vegetable fibers, is stronger and more manageable when damp. The moisture causes the fiber ends to stick together and twist into the yarn being formed, acting as a lubricant in much the same way as does oil with sheep's wool. Dry spun flax is uneven and hairy. Traditionally, saliva was used for moisture, and there are literary references to foul mouths as a result of spinning flax. Most spinners today keep a little cup of water nearby—some spinning wheels have a special place for a water cup. As the twist runs up the drafted fibers, the thumb and index finger move up with it, and the moistened fiber ends are laid smoothly in.

Although it is possible to prepare the fiber from the raw plant, flax is available in the form of tow, combed sliver, and line. Usually it is good quality, often coming from Belgium or Ireland, where flax is still cultivated commercially. Tow can be carded with wood cards or spun directly from the

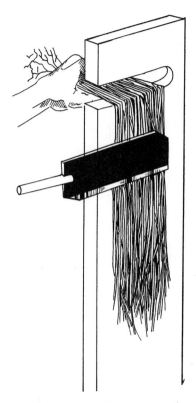

Scutching. Scutching was traditionally done over the end of a securely braced hardwood board about 3 feet high. A hand-held paddlelike knife, called the scutching knife, comes down at an angle against the flax as the free hand moves the fibers back and forth.

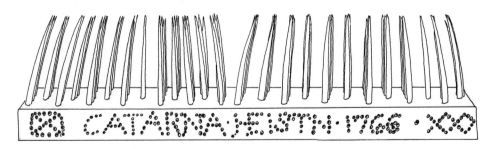

Hackling. The flax hackle—the one illustrated is an eighteenth-century Pennsylvania German hackle—is usually a piece of hardwood about 10" long, 5" wide, and 1" thick with a hundred or more sharp, projecting iron spikes 3 to 4" in length. The flax hackle is a simple tool, found wherever linen yarns are found. The inscription, done in perforated tin and mounted on the wood, bears out the regional or ethnic tradition. The flax hackle was symbolic of the male-female relationship, characteristic of a successful marriage—it was often made during courtship, with the two names and the marriage date inscribed as the symbol of joining and partnership. The first stages of flax preparation involve brute force. Once the flax reaches the hackle, a light hand takes over and carries the fibers on through hackling, spinning, and weaving.

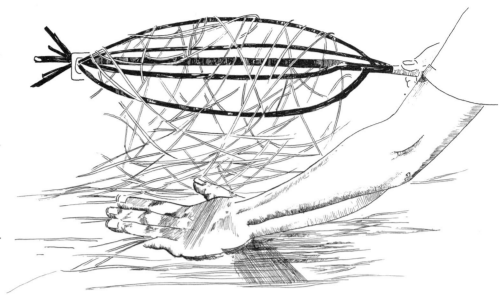

Line flax is composed of long fibers that can be spun into a fine, strong linen thread. One way to handle these long fibers is to mount them on a distaff. A distaff can be made from a branch by gathering the twigs together as shown in the illustration. Loosen the fibers, and lay them out on a table. Slowly turn the distaff and catch a few of the fibers, which will draw other fibers. Keep turning until the distaff is loaded with fibers and looks like a cocoon. The distaff may be held under the arm or mounted.

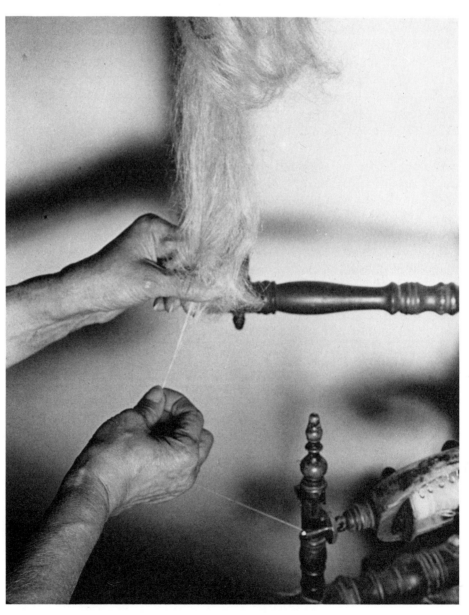

Spinning flax from distaff to wheel. Draw the flax fibers down from the distaff, and allow them to feed into the wheel orifice. The right hand smoothes the yarn and controls the twist.

mass. Fibers are usually short and coarse, and produce a textured, weak yarn.

Most often flax is available in a form developed for commercial spinners. The fibers are cut up into lengths of 3 to 5", carded, and then drawn into a combed top or sliver. The sliver sometimes comes with an artificial crimp that helps keep the fibers together and keeps them from sliding past one another. The crimp is put in to facilitate mill spinning on machines designed for wool and disappears as soon as the fibers are pulled apart. Lengths of sliver should be divided depending on the size yarn desired, but otherwise it is ready to spin. If the fibers were predominately high quality before cutting, the yarn produced can be fine, smooth, and strong.

Line flax (usually in lengths of 20 to 30") is not for the beginner—it requires special attention. Generally speaking, long fibers make for a stronger, more lustrous yarn, but they tangle easily. If they are too long to be drafted, they must be pulled in such a way as to come in order and not tangle.

Since Roman times, a distaff has been used to hold the flax fibers that are about to be spun. Whether hand held, attached to the wheel, or standing alone, the distaff is set up on the spinner's left. To spin the flax, dampen your left thumb and forefinger and pull down a few fibers with your left hand. As you slowly treadle, your left and right hands should alternate. As your left hand draws gently down, the right hand smoothes the yarn, moving up with the twist and then taking over from the left hand as the fingers are moistened again. Be careful to keep the twist from running too high and tangling into the distaff. Treat the fine, long fibers lightly and slowly. After a while,

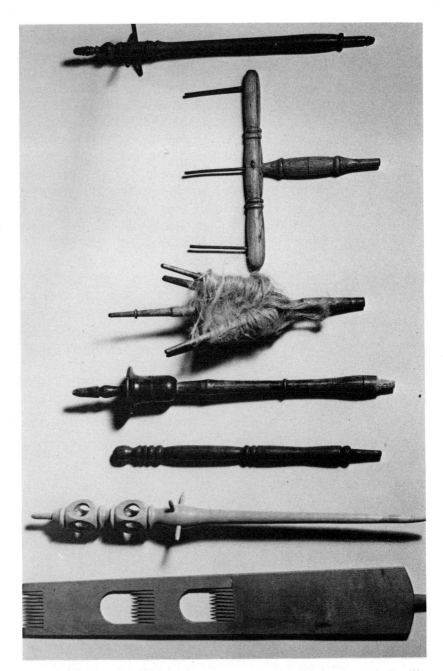

Distaffs for holding flax fibers come in various sizes and shapes—each distaff shown is designed to fit on a spinning wheel. The long flax fibers are arranged so they are loosely held to allow the spinner to draw down just enough for the forming yarn. A silk ribbon is frequently used to help secure the fibers. The second distaff from the top is called a tow fork. The short, coarse flax fibers left over after hackling—the tow—are formed into a roving, which is wound over and under the distaff prongs. These short fibers are spun much like wool, except water is used to make the fibers manageable.

turn the distaff to keep its load balanced. The hand motions are different from those used when spinning from a combed top or rolag. The left hand pulls out and down—if it pulls back, tangles occur. Many old spinning wheels were specifically designed for flax. They frequently have a built-in distaff arranged on the spinner's left. Tall floor distaffs and distaffs held under the arm or in the belt were also used with flax.

One of the simplest methods of spinning line flax is to take the hank, or part of it, tie it securely but loosely at one end, and suspend it above the wheel orifice near your left shoulder. Then pull the fibers down as needed. The flax can be suspended from a tree branch, a rafter, or some kind of pole ar-

rangement. The tie at the top will have to be periodically adjusted.

Line flax can be spun without a distaff or special suspension arrangement by simply dividing the hank into a number of very thin slivers so a minimum amount of drafting is needed during spinning. The hands work very far apart, with an exceptionally long drafting area in order for the long fibers to attenuate.

NETTLES

For thousands of years, fibers from the stems of various nettle plants have been used for spinning. Ramie, sometimes called China Grass, is obtained from the bast of the stingless nettles (*Bochmeria nivea*), woody Asian plants with broad leaves. The plant, which was used

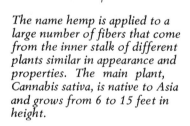

The name hemp is applied to a large number of fibers that come from the inner stalk of different plants similar in appearance and properties. The main plant, Cannabis sativa, is native to Asia and grows from 6 to 15 feet in height.

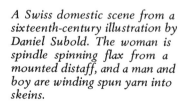

A Swiss domestic scene from a sixteenth-century illustration by Daniel Subold. The woman is spindle spinning flax from a mounted distaff, and a man and boy are winding spun yarn into skeins.

as a fiber source in ancient China, grows so rapidly that the stalks, shooting up from a tap root, can be cut at least three times in one year. The stems are cut when mature, and the leaves and branches stripped. Raw ramie contains gums that hold the fibers together, and they can be removed by chemical action (caustic soda) or much hand labor. Ramie has not proven an economically successful fiber, since the fibers come in various lengths and require sorting or cutting.

This fiber is lustrous, pure white, very strong, and highly resistent to mildew, heat, and bacteria. It is very inelastic and spins into a somewhat brittle yarn. The structure of the fiber is similar to that of flax, but the surface is smoother and more regular, giving a high luster because of the broader reflective surface. The broader surface also means that the fiber has little cohesive quality and that, even though the fibers are fine and long, a fine yarn cannot be spun from them because the fibers will not hold the twist. Combed ramie is available to the handspinner and can be spun like the combed flax sliver. It feels very soft and silky, but spins into a firm yarn which will be smooth if wet spun.

The stinging nettle (*Urtica Species*), common in the United States, has also been used at different times as a fiber source. The fiber is extracted from the stem of the plant in the same manner used in processing flax. The fiber is long and soft and resistent to moisture, but comparatively weak. Each plant yields only a small amount of usable fiber, which means a lot of work for little return. The leaves of the plant are covered with hairs that secrete a stinging fluid which affects the skin on contact, so gathering and handling the plant is particularly unpleasant.

HEMP

Hemp is a bast fiber and handled in the same way as flax. Hemp was unknown to the Egyptians and to early central and western Europe—its use spread east from the Caspian Sea area, and it was used very early in India and China. It figures in early Japanese mythology and is considered the oldest cultivated textile plant in Japan. It is now grown in temperate and tropical areas all over the world. The best quality comes, as it always has, from the Orient. Hemp lacks the fineness of better quality flax—since the Middle Ages in Europe, clothes of hemp have always been a sign of poverty. Hemp is used primarily for cord, ropes, and rough cloths. It is light brown in color and cannot be bleached without damaging the fibers.

Compared to flax, hemp is a robust and tough plant, with stalks reaching 10 feet or more. It takes more time to mature (four to five months) and requires higher summer temperatures than flax, but is much hardier. It does not deplete the soil to the extent that flax does. Hemp requires soft, rich, moist soil or lots of fertilizer. It is easy to grow, and, if it is properly planted, it can be forgotten about until it is ready for cutting. The plant grows and develops so quickly that weeds don't stand a chance in competition with it. If the seeds are planted too close, the stalks will be spindly. If they are too far apart, they will overdevelop, and the fibers will become coarse. Unlike flax, hemp has separate male and female plants. The female plant is stronger and more robust and is picked later than the male, allowing the seeds to ripen. Some people find the harvesting unpleasant because the plants have a strong smell. The leaves and flowers are sometimes

The jute plant reaches a height of from 6 to 15 feet and has a thick fibrous inner layer that produces two to five times as much fiber as a flax plant. The fiber is coarse and bulky compared to flax.

dried and smoked as marijuana, and for this reason many governments have outlawed its cultivation.

Hemp is harvested by cutting, and it then goes through the same rigorous treatment as flax. Retting takes longer: 10 days for the male and three weeks for the female. The retting water becomes so polluted that it is used as an insecticide. After breaking, scutching, and hackling, the final product—when compared to flax—is stiff and harsh, with little pliability. Structurally, hemp is similar to flax, with a joint-like structure that takes the twist of spinning nicely. The fibers are strong and resistant to rotting. Hemp is usually available in sliver form and is spun like short-fibered flax.

JUTE

Jute is another bast fiber. The plant, which includes various species of *Corchorus*, has been grown in India since remote times. It is a bulky, cheap, lustrous fiber and has been traditionally used for crude, coarse clothes and expendable items, such as sacks and packing material. It is grown so cheaply in India and Pakistan that it is not often commercially cultivated elsewhere. The plant requires a great deal of moisture and just the right exposure to sunlight for proper fiber growth. It reaches a height of 6 to 15 feet and has a very thick fibrous layer—two to five times as much fiber as the flax plant provides. If the crop is not cut before the seeds ripen, the fiber quality deteriorates. It is retted and stripped in the same manner as flax. The fibrous strands vary in length and are usually cut into manageable lengths for spinning.

Jute has a hard, smooth surface, without the irregularities necessary for good spinning qualities. It is also somewhat woody and, conse-

quently, harsh and hard on the hands. It has a beautiful luster that excites many spinners and weavers, and, since it is cheap, it can be spun into bulky, lustrous yarns for decorative forms or wall hangings. It can be carded and spun in its natural state to produce a hairy yarn. If oil and water are added to lubricate the fibers before carding, the fibers will spin more easily and a smooth, even yarn can be formed. The fibers are inelastic and not very durable—they deteriorate rapidly when exposed to moisture. Thus jute is ill-suited for much beyond decorative or temporary uses.

LEAF FIBERS

Leaf fibers come from the inner parts of fleshy, long leaves. They are usually long, hard, resistant fibers that are obtained by peeling away the outside layer of the leaf, scraping the inner part, and then stripping away the fibers. They are generally used for ropes and baskets. Leaf fibers are thicker and stiffer than the bast fibers. They spin into a rough yarn and are best spun with the use of water. The fibers can be drawn down from a suspended bundle as with line flax, or cut and then spun. Shorter fibers can also be carded.

The primary leaf fibers are the agave fibers, primarily from Mexico, which are frequently called sisal; abaca from the musa plant, native to the Philippines and frequently called manila hemp; and New Zealand flax. The leaf fibers of the New Zealand flax plant were used by the Maoris long before the white man arrived in New Zealand. Today the plant is widely cultivated in California. Other leaf fibers are pina, from the leaves of the pineapple plant, which produces a fine, silky, lustrous fiber; and raffia, from the leaves of the raffia palm, which is also used for textiles.

The Musa plant produces abaca, another leaf fiber. It is native to the Philippines and related to the banana plant. The plant grows as suckers from a short rootstock to a height of from 10 to 25 feet. The fiber is coarse, strong, and resistant to both fresh and salt water.

Many spinners are no longer interested in spinning fine, soft, perfect yarns, but are interested rather in the coarse fibers that produce stiff, textured yarns, which can give body and stability to wall hangings and new life and variety to tapestry work. Many of the cheap vegetable fibers provide a source that has been untapped by spinners.

Using these fibers entails using either large orifice wheels or a spike quill wheel, since the stiff, inflexible fibers will get caught on flyer hooks. Spinning these heavier fibers usually requires a very sturdy wheel to provide the force and energy to keep the twist going up the heavy yarns.

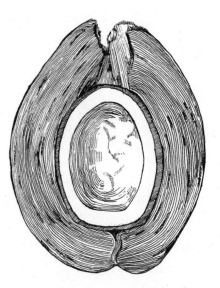

The husk of the coconut produces a reddish brown, coarse fiber of variable strength that is highly resistant to rot. The husks are separated from the nuts, retted—usually in salt water for five to six months—and then dried and beaten. Only a very crude, stiff cord can be spun from the husk. The bark of the tree is also used as a fiber source.

The leaves of the henequen of Yucatan provide one of the main sources of agave fibers. The leaves are cut periodically over a 12-year period. The fiber, frequently referred to as sisal or Yucatan sisal, is golden-white in color and is scraped from inside the leaves.

CHAPTER NINE

Silk Fiber

In the silkworm month we trim the mulberry trees.
  Taking those axes and hatchets,
  We top off the higher boughs,
  And strip the young ones of their leaves.
  In the seventh month the shrikes cry,
  In the eighth month we tend to spinning
  Of both dark and yellow silk.
Most becoming is the silk I dye bright red,
Which I shall make into a cloak for my lord.

In the Seventh Month
Shih Ching
Chinese 12th century B.C.
Translated by Irving Y. Lo

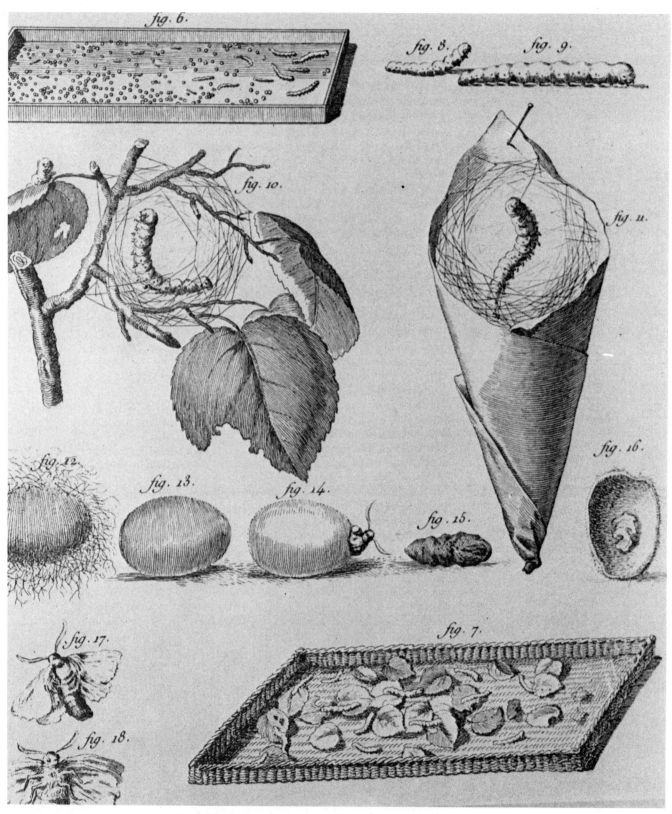

The silkworm begins its short life cycle as a small egg and rapidly grows to a large worm, which spins a protective coating, or cocoon, of silk. The worm changes into a moth within the cocoon and emerges to mate and lay eggs. (A Diderot Pictorial Encyclopedia of Trades and Industry.)

Silk is an ancient fiber—luxurious, mysterious, awe inspiring, and always the property and symbol of the powerful and wealthy. Silk strands are the product, strangely, of the lowly worm, and the necessarily complex procedure that transforms the continuous filament extruded by a worm into fabric fit for kings and emperors is both technically complex and historically fascinating.

Silk first appears as the extrusion of the worm as it binds itself into the protection of the cocoon that will house and protect it during the pupal, or metamorphic, stage of its development. All true silkworms belong to the general class *Lepidoptera*—scale-winged insects. The main genus is *Bombyx* and the principal species is the *Bombyx mori*. *Mori* means belonging to the mulberry tree, and the *Bombyx mori* feeds only on mulberry leaves. This silkworm is completely domesticated and requires constant

human care from the time the eggs are laid until the cocoons are ready for reeling or spinning. The *Bombyx mori* lives for less than two months, during which it goes through a complete metamorphosis from egg to larva, to pupa, to moth. The *Bombyx mori* has been so fully domesticated that as a worm it does not move far and as a moth it cannot fly. Without constant human care, the species would perish.

Eggs are readily available, and the silkworm makes excellent material for close observation and study. Raising silkworms is also a way of producing fibers that are especially enjoyable for spinning. And, the silkworm requires only two things: constant care and mulberry leaves.

Silk that is reeled from perfect cocoons as a continuous filament is not spun in the traditional sense, but merely twisted to give strength. However, the imperfect cocoons

Spinning tussah, or wild, silk fibers on the Ashford spinning wheel. The loom in the background is warped with handspun silk for a 10 foot wide blanket.

and parts that are left over after reeling are broken into shorter fibers, which are first subjected to the same cleaning and combing processes that are used on wool and cotton and then made into spun silk. This so-called silk waste, as well as "wild" silk from undomesticated worms, is available to the handspinner in many forms through spinning suppliers.

There are many other worms besides the *Bombyx mori* that are important silk producers. However, they are not capable of being domesticated or artificially cultivated and exist only in the wild. These creatures live and build their cocoons in such places as oak trees, castor-oil plants, cherry trees, and

mulberry trees. Their silk is called wild, or tussah, silk. Wild silk is sturdier, coarser, and not as soft or lustrous as domesticated silk. It is usually honey colored and very beautiful. Handspinners prize it highly and take great pleasure in its subtle shades and opalescent qualities.

This chapter on silk offers a brief attempt to unwind the mystery of silk; to delve into the traditional aspects of this rare and costly fiber; and to give helpful and specific information on rearing and caring for silkworms at home or in the classroom.

HISTORY

From the beginning in China, silk was a luxury fiber that excited the hand and the eye and stood above all others in beauty and desirability. The silk industry began in ancient China and is traced back to 2640

B.C. Its origins and use are imbued with mythology and tradition. At times, the brilliant and costly fiber was reserved exclusively for the emperor, and, for many more years, it was used only by those of noble birth. The Chinese kept the secret of silk well and monopolized its production for thousands of years. Silk was always an important trade commodity, and, in China, taxes were often paid with silk. Silk became a medium of exchange. By 126 B.C., Tartar caravans were transporting silk over the mountains and deserts to Persia, Syria, and Arabia over the "Silk Road," the longest trade route in the ancient world, which extended for more than 6,000 miles. Western traders bartered for the silk in Damascus, where it was as precious as gold.

Seres—from sericulture, the raising of silkworms—eventually became a Greek word for Chinese, so closely was silk associated with China. By the beginning of the Christian era, raw silk from the Orient was a highly desired and costly item. During this period, and into modern times, clothing for everyday use was produced within the communities and families of those who wore it. By contrast, when it came to the luxury of silk, no risk or cost was too great. Silk, which was light, colorful, brilliant, and in every way special, was highly prized as a symbol of influence, wealth, and prestige.

During the early Christian era sericulture spread first to Japan and then gradually through Central Asia, Persia, and Turkey. By the

The body of the fully developed silkworm (left) has 13 segments in addition to a small head with feelers and six pairs of eyes. The mouth, located in the center of the head (on the right), contains sharp teeth for eating mulberry leaves. Below the mouth is a large protuberance called the spinner, through which the silk fluid passes as the worm spins its cocoon. The silk moth (above) is about 1" in length and whitish in color. The female moth is larger than the male.

thirteenth century, there were silk centers in Greece, Sicily, Italy, Spain, France, and Russia. Silk in the form of *Bombyx mori* was carried to all parts of the world. In some places, the climate was not suitable for mulberry trees, and, in other areas, the tedious and highly skilled labor required of silkworkers was not available at any price. Silkworms were first brought to Mexico in 1531 by Cortes, but any likeness of a silk industry there died out by the seventeenth century. King James I was very anxious to start a silk industry in England but failed—partially because the mulberry trees did not do well in the English climate, but also for economic and political reasons. He sent shipments of eggs and trees to America in the early seventeenth century, hoping that sericulture would replace the "pernicious and offensive weed tobacco." Under James I, silk production in colonial America was encouraged by subsidies, rewards, release from taxes, and by the "propaganda" of the written word:

Where Wormes and food doe naturally abound
A gallant Silken Trade must there be found.
Virginia excels the World in both—
Envie nor malice can gaine say this troth!

But while silk centers flourished in Byzantium, Italy, and France, sericulture did not become firmly established in America. The tedious, time-consuming work that required cheap but skilled labor did not find a home in America. Today, Japan remains the primary producer and consumer of silk. The Japanese machinery, family structure, attitude, and tradition provide a proper atmosphere for the economic success of sericulture in that country.

CHARACTERISTICS OF SILK

Unlike wool or cotton, silk is not cellular in structure. It is a long, continuous, fine filament composed almost entirely of protein. Although silk does not grow on the back of an animal, it too is basically a protective coating, is a natural insulator, and is comfortable at any temperature. Silk has great tensile strength and good elasticity; it is the strongest of all natural fibers, but the lightest in weight strand for strand—the tensile strength of silk is equal to that of steel. Aside from fineness and strength, the most striking physical property of silk, especially of reeled silk, is its high luster. Silk is a very smooth, clean fiber that does not hold dust, dirt, or moisture, and so is very easy to care for. It does not burn easily, resists creases, drapes beautifully, and has a great affinity for dyes. There are frequent references in Roman literature to the transparency of silk and to the way it reveals the body. The emperor Augustus in 14 A.D. forbade the wearing of silk for men, on the basis that "silk degrades a man."

Silk that is not reeled is cut up into convenient spinning lengths, but the shorter the fibers the less strength, luster, and fineness of the spun yarn. The combination of strength (which allows for fineness in fabrics), elasticity, and shimmer as well as its rarity and cost makes silk a very special fiber, appropriate for use in the most highly exalted places.

SERICULTURE IN CHINA AND JAPAN

Silk production is very important in the history of China and Japan and is treated with reverence in the literature and art of these countries.

Each spring before the first crop of eggs hatches, special blessings are

Red embroidered carpet:
Selected cocoons are firm dressed and boiled in clear water;
The choicest silk, thus reeled, is soaked in safflower juice;
Then the fibers, dyed more reddish than blue,
Are woven into a carpet for the Hall of Spreading Fragrance.

Fragrance-spreading hall is over a hundred feet long,
The embroidered carpet barely enough to cover the floor,
Silk of brightest sheen is fine and soft, and the fragrance
     wafts in the breeze.
Delicate threads, embossed flowers, can hardly stand the weight,
As beautiful ladies come treading on it, singing and dancing;
Their gauze stockings and embroidered shoes sink with every step.

The carpet from T'ai-yüan is coarse, its fabric hard;
The quilt from Ch'eng-tu is thin, its brocaded flowers cold—
How could they compare with this carpet, warm and soft?

Every year, in the tenth month, when orders come to Hsüan-chou,
The Governor has the carpet woven in a new elegant design,
Stating that, as His Majesty's servant, he knows how to do his best.
When a hundred men together carry it into the palace,
The fabric is so thick, the silk so lavish, that it can't even be rolled.

Governor of Hsüan-chou, don't you know:
One carpet ten feet long—
A thousand ounces of silk thread?
The floor may not feel cold but people need warmth,
Please be sparing in robbing people of clothes to cover the ground!

The Red Embroidered Carpet
Po Chü-yi
Chinese 772-846 B.C.
(Tr. Wu-Chi Liu)

invoked and ceremonies performed to insure success.

Photographs of a group of wood-cut prints by the eighteenth-century Japanese artist Kitagawa Utamaro (1753–1806) are shown as an introduction to the steps involved in sericulture (pages 187–195).

RAISING SILKWORMS ON A SMALL SCALE

Silkworms can be raised easily wherever there is access to mulberry trees. Many people raise silkworms to gain insight into the life of this incredible insect; others raise them for the silk fibers that can be reeled or spun. Many spinners who are not in a position to have sheep or grow flax or cotton raise silkworms. It is one way to become intimate with a fiber source. The entire process takes less than two months and can be done easily in the home or classroom. Raising silkworms on a small scale requires no special equipment and involves little expense. In an age where everything is purchased in stores, it is occasionally useful to be reminded of the miracle of creation. I can think of no better way of doing it then by observing the silkworm.

Within its short life, the silk-worm accomplishes a complete metamorphosis: from egg to larva, to pupa, to moth. After the eggs hatch, the larva pass through four "molts" during their development, shedding their skins in order to permit growth, and eventually increasing 10,000 times in weight. John Chrysostom, patriarch of Constantinople from 398-404 A.D., described the development of the silkworm in great detail, because the transformations of the animal seemed to him a perfect analogy to the internal transformations of the human soul.

The information in this section on raising silkworms comes from many sources, but primarily from the notes of Fumiko Pentler, who before her death spent many years raising and studying silkworms.

To begin the silk cycle, silkworm eggs must be obtained. Addresses and sources are listed at the back of this book. It takes approximately 30 days from the time the eggs hatch until the cocoons are ready to spin. Treat the eggs and worms with the utmost care and sensitivity. Keep them in partial darkness, and protect them from direct sunlight, drafts, and excessive moisture. Be careful to keep the surrounding area clean, and try to maintain even temperatures. Mulberry leaves are of course a necessity. The worms are very particular and will not accept substitutes. For your first experiment, use only a few eggs, about 20 or 30. The cycle goes like clockwork, so keep careful records of growth and activity.

Until you are ready to begin, keep the silkworm eggs in an air-tight container in the vegetable compartment of the refrigerator (40° to 45°F.). To begin the cycle, take a small plastic container that has a cover. Line the bottom with a paper towel, and place the eggs on the towel. In dry places, the eggs will need additional moisture. Take a small piece of aluminum foil, and place a little piece of moist cotton batting on it. Put this inside the box near the eggs. If the eggs are kept at 70°F. with approximately 85% humidity, they should hatch in 8 to 12 days. However, incubation can take from a few days to a month. Be sure to put the lid on in such a way as to allow for air circulation—this keeps the leaves and cotton from drying out too rapidly.

The newly hatched worms are black and hairy and will immediately begin eating. To feed them, soak the mulberry leaves in water until they become turgid, and then wash and dry them. Leaves will keep in the refrigerator (vegetable compartment) for about a week. The newly hatched worms require pieces of tender young leaves. As they increase in size, the worms will eat the tougher parts, and, eventually, they will eat whole leaves. During this early period, fresh leaf pieces should be given to the worms every 4 hours. Uneaten leaves should be removed and the paper towel periodically changed. To change paper towels, put a fresh piece of tender mulberry leaf near the hatching eggs. The worms will crawl to the top of the leaf, and you can then change the towel.

The first larval stage takes 4 days, and goes from the time the eggs hatch until the first molt, when the worms become very quiet and do not eat for about 14 to 20 hours. When the worms become active again, they shed their black skins—the new skins are lighter in color.

The second larval stage is a period of 3 to 5 days between the first and second molts. Maintain the same temperature and humidity as before. As the worms grow, their

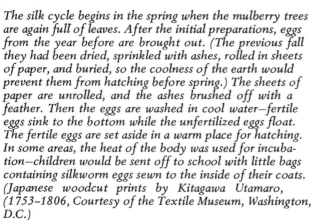

The silk cycle begins in the spring when the mulberry trees are again full of leaves. After the initial preparations, eggs from the year before are brought out. (The previous fall they had been dried, sprinkled with ashes, rolled in sheets of paper, and buried, so the coolness of the earth would prevent them from hatching before spring.) The sheets of paper are unrolled, and the ashes brushed off with a feather. Then the eggs are washed in cool water—fertile eggs sink to the bottom while the unfertilized eggs float. The fertile eggs are set aside in a warm place for hatching. In some areas, the heat of the body was used for incubation—children would be sent off to school with little bags containing silkworm eggs sewn to the inside of their coats. (Japanese woodcut prints by Kitagawa Utamaro, (1753–1806, Courtesy of the Textile Museum, Washington, D.C.)

As the eggs are incubating, young leaves and buds are picked from the mulberry trees. This tree is indigenous to China and thrives in many other parts of the world. Fresh, tender leaves must be available, as the silkworms are very particular and will not consume older, tougher leaves.

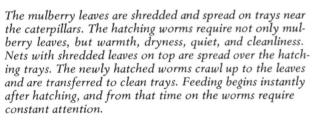

The mulberry leaves are shredded and spread on trays near the caterpillars. The hatching worms require not only mulberry leaves, but warmth, dryness, quiet, and cleanliness. Nets with shredded leaves on top are spread over the hatching trays. The newly hatched worms crawl up to the leaves and are transferred to clean trays. Feeding begins instantly after hatching, and from that time on the worms require constant attention.

The worms are transferred from tray to tray as they rapidly grow from the size of a pinpoint to about 3" in length. As the worms grow, the number of trays needed multiplies, and, as the worms get larger, more and more mulberry leaves are needed.

tough skins become tightly stretched. At the end of this stage, the worms again stop eating and become inactive for about 22 hours prior to shedding their skins.

The third larval stage is the period between the second and third molts and lasts for about 4 days. Ideally, the temperature should be a little cooler (77°) and the humidity a little less (80%). The worms grow very rapidly at this stage. Larger or more containers are necessary, and larger, tougher parts of leaves may be provided. The paper towels should be changed daily, and uneaten leaves and droppings should be removed. The third molt usually lasts longer than the second.

The fourth larval stage lasts for 4 to 5 days. The ideal temperature is 75° with 70% humidity. At the end of this period, the worms enter their longest period of inactivity, which lasts about 40 hours. Then they molt for the final time, beginning the last stage of larval growth, which lasts for about 7 days. The temperature and humidity should be dropped, if possible, to 73° and 70% humidity. At this stage, the moist cotton is unnecessary. The worms consume leaves at a rapid rate and must be fed frequently. The body of the fully developed silkworm is almost white in color. It is about 3" in length and has 13 segments in addition to its head. When the silkworms are ready to spin their cocoons, they stop eating and become very still. They become light amber in color and almost translucent. The folds between their segments become more pronounced, and their bodies shorter. When they begin to wave their heads from side to side, they are ready to spin.

In the silkworm's early stages, the digestive tract occupies the greater part of the body. The silk glands, which produce the material for the silk filaments, are located directly under the digestive tract, one on each side of the worm. As the worm eats and grows, the silk glands swell, occupying more and more of the body. They fill with the fluid that will be later extruded as silk. The main component of silk, a protein called fibroin, is produced in the rear portion of the silk glands. The fluid passes into the middle part of the gland, where it is coated with a sticky, gluelike substance called sericin. This coated substance then goes into the forward part of the silk gland near the head of the worm. Then the two soft filaments—one from each gland, and each filament with its fibroin core and sericin coating—enter the spinning organ, called the spinneret. The two soft filaments are pressed out of the spinneret together as a single strand. They quickly harden when exposed to air. The sericin coating helps hold the cocoon together and keeps it in shape.

An egg carton makes an ideal place for cocoon spinning. When the silkworms are ready to spin, place a worm in each cell of the egg carton. A piece of mulberry leaf can also be put in just in case the worm wants to eat. Saran wrap or wax paper can be loosely placed over the top to protect the worms and to keep them in place. Clear plastic boxes with cubicles or branches can also be used for cocoon anchoring. Be sure to mark down the date when each worm begins spinning.

While spinning, the silkworm moves its head in a figure-eight motion. The worm first spins anchoring threads and then spins for about 12 hours, constructing a thin-walled cocoon. At this point, it excretes urine and feces to the outside. The worm then resumes

After about 30 days, the caterpillars stop eating and become motionless. The time for cocoon spinning is near. They are placed on grids constructed of bamboo, with branches of rice straw that give the caterpillars anchor points for their cocoons. Each worm or caterpillar finds a comfortable spot and begins to spin a silk cocoon.

The caterpillar rests in its pupal stage from 15 to 17 days, changing from a caterpillar into a moth. A few of the cocoons are selected for breeding, but most of the pupae are killed by treating the cocoons with heat. This prevents the moth from emerging and breaking the continuous silk filament.

spinning to make a hard, tight cocoon. It spins day and night for a total of 60 hours or more. The cocoon is one single, continuous thread, usually half a mile or more in length. Excessive moisture and temperatures above 79° during spinning may result in cocoons that are difficult to reel. The cocoons will be white, gold, beige, or some other color, depending on the strain of the silkworms. Each cocoon is a hard, compact shell, sometimes constricted in the middle. It is much shorter than the original length of the silkworm, and generally measures about 1½" in length and about ¾" in width.

After the cocoon is completed, the silkworm begins its transformation into a pupa, and sheds its old skin inside the cocoon. The pupal stage lasts for about 15 days. The cocoons should not be handled for the first 10 days. During this period, the skin of the pupa hardens—if the cocoons are handled, the pupa might be injured and the blood will stain the cocoon.

After 10 days, select the best cocoons for breeding. It is, of course, necessary to have both male and female moths for egg production, so do not take only the largest—males usually make smaller cocoons. Since the female will lay many hundreds of eggs, only a few cocoons need to be set aside for breeding. The other cocoons must be heat-treated to kill the pupa, since if left alive it will change into a moth and break the continuous filament. Hold the cocoons at room temperature for a total of 13 days, measured from the time when each silkworm first began to spin its cocoon. Then spread the cocoons on a thick layer of newspapers on the top of a cookie sheet, and heat them in an oven for about 3 hours at between 214° and 225°F. After this heat treatment, allow the co-

coons to cool and place them in a plastic bag for future use. The cocoons will remain in good condition for a long time at room temperature. At the end of the 13-day period, the cocoons can also be stored in the refrigerator for a short time while other cocoons are maturing. All the cocoons can then be plunged into a pan of boiling water for 10 minutes and reeled immediately. The hot water will kill the pupa.

When the time comes for the breeder moths to emerge—usually on the morning of the 15th day—place the cocoons in a box. Early in the morning, the pupa casts off its skin to become a moth. The moth moistens one end of the cocoon with enzymes, which dissolve the silk fibers, and then pushes its way through the resulting small round hole. After emerging, the moth pumps fluid into its folded wings and spreads them out. The moths cannot fly or eat. They are about 1" in length and whitish in color with pale brown bars on the upper wings. The moths will mate almost immediately—the females are larger, and exude a perfume which instantly attracts the male. The male will die shortly after mating, and the female shortly after laying her eggs. After mating, place the female moth on a piece of plastic food wrap. Over a 3-day period, she will lay several hundred eggs of pinpoint size, with slight depressions in the center. The sticky eggs hold to the paper, which can be rolled (eggs inside) and placed in a sealed bottle. Keep the eggs in the vegetable compartment of the refrigerator at 40° to 45°F. until you are now ready to go through the cycle again.

Raising silkworms can keep life very interesting. Margherite Shimmin of Pasadena, California, who supplies silkworm eggs to

The moths mate almost immediately after emerging from the cocoons that have been set aside for breeding.

Today's silkworm moth cannot fly. The male moth dies a few days after mating, and the female expires immediately after laying her eggs, which will be set aside for the next crop of silkworms. In Japan, there are usually three silkworm crops a year—spring, summer, and fall. Other species of silkworms that are found in the wild will live on as moths for weeks before dying.

handspinners, writes of one such experience.

One year, after we had stashed in our refrigerator the matured eggs of a tropical variety (no diapause!), somehow something spilled and wet all the eggs (laid on paper towels). Knowing they would rot unless quickly dried, I started taking them out to dry, one group at a time. In every case several—many!—little worms hatched before the paper was dry! I replaced the dry ones in the refrigerator as fast as possible, but ere they were all dried, and put back under refrigeration, we had 2,651 worms to feed! We scrounged mulberry leaves from wherever we could find any. And as they became ready to spin, there were boxes, cartons, and whatever might be handy, all over tables and floors, full of ravenously appetited and/or spinning caterpillars!

PREPARING SILK FOR REELING AND SPINNING

Silk that still contains the gum-coating sericin is called raw silk. Sericin makes up about 25% of the total weight, and makes the silk feel harsh and stiff. Even after reeling, much of the sericin remains. The luster and softness characteristic of silk comes only after the removal of the sericin. This process is a scouring operation, and is referred to as discharging, stripping, or degumming. Perfect cocoons are usually reeled—rather than spun—to maintain the character of the continuous filament, but many handspinners do not have the patience or interest for the tedious work of reeling. They break all their cocoons down into short fiber lengths for spun silk.

To reel silk, take 8 to 12 cocoons and pour boiling water over them. Gently press the cocoons down to keep them submerged. The hot water softens the sericin so the silk filaments can be reeled without breaking. As the water cools, the vacuum will pull water into the cocoons. This added weight makes it easier to keep them in the water during reeling. At first, it will seem as though there are many ends on each cocoon, but, as the fuzz coating comes off, a single filament will remain.

Combine the 8 to 12 filaments together, and reel the thread off on to a piece of cardboard. An individual strand is very fine and almost invisible, which is why a number of filaments are reeled together. The water temperature should be kept warm, about 175°F., to prevent the sericin from hardening. If one of the filaments breaks, add it back in. At the beginning end where the worm began the cocoon, the filament is larger in diameter. At the other end, where the strength of the worm decreased and the supply of the silk fluid began to diminish, the diameter is thinner. The filament for the best grade of silk, called organzine, is taken in one unbroken length from the center portion of the cocoon. Ten pounds of cocoons are usually required for one pound of reeled raw silk.

The "throwing" of reeled silk is done to give strength and bulk to the thread. It is traditionally done on a simple quilltype wheel. The term is derived from the Anglo-Saxon word "thrawan," which means "to twist." The exact amount of doubling and twisting depends upon the strength and texture desired. Since these are parallel, continuous filaments, there is no spinning in the traditional sense.

Only perfect cocoons can be reeled. All other silk—including partially spun cocoons, stained cocoons, those which are soft, mis-

The finest quality silk is reeled from perfect cocoons. The cocoons are first placed in boiling water for about 10 minutes to dissolve the gummy substance that surrounds the silk filament. As the cocoon softens, the long, continuous filament loosens and the end comes free. A single strand is too thin for any practical use, so 5 to 12 cocoons must be unwound simultaneously to form the continuous thread.

After reeling, the skeins of silk are scoured, washed, stretched, and hung up to dry. In the woodcut, the filaments are not delineated.

The silk thread is sometimes twisted or doubled to give it strength and texture. This process, called throwing, is very much like spinning. Warp threads are then mounted on the loom in preparation for weaving.

The silk threads are woven into fabrics on the traditional Japanese silk loom. (Japanese woodcut prints by Kitagawa Utamaro, 1753–1806, Courtesy of the Textile Museum, Washington, D.C.)

Fumiko Pentler reeling silk cocoons on to a traditional Japanese silk reel.

A front view of the traditional Japanese silk reel shown in the previous illustration. The silk filaments travel from the cocoons over a spool and up through a little metal hoop to the reel. As the handle on the left is turned to rotate the reel, the metal hoop moves back and forth so the silk winds evenly along the width of the bobbin.

shapen, or not uniformly spun, as well as all the bits and pieces of fiber left over from reeling or strands used to anchor cocoons—is subjected to the same cleaning and combing processes that are used on wool. These miscellaneous fibers are spun just like wool or any other shorter fiber to make spun silk threads or yarns.

When the gluelike sericin that coats the silk filaments is boiled and scoured off, the double thread spun by the worm separates and the silk appears as single, lustrous, almost white filaments. Cocoons and fibers can be cut to manageable lengths or pulled apart either before or after scouring. To remove the sericin, submerge the silk in hot, soapy water. Use soft water and a mild soap that is free from alkaline carbonates. Keep the solution at about 195°F. for at least 1 hour, and then rinse the silk. The soapy solution will become thick with sericin. Traditionally, the solution is saved and added to the silk dye bath, where it aids in uniform dyeing. A solution of water, hydrosulfite (not more than 3%) and ivory flakes simmered with the silk immersed for a couple of hours also works well. Depending on the amount of sericin, the scouring process can be repeated. After scouring, the silk fibers should be white, soft, and lustrous.

Silk waste, or fibers that for one reason or another are not reeled, come to the handspinner in various forms from commercial outlets. Usually the sericin is removed. Sometimes matted cocoons and remnants are stretched and drawn over a frame to arrange the fibers in the form of 10" square soft sheets called batts. These batts are sometimes used as a stuffing between the outer fabric and lining, when exceptional warmth is required. To spin from these batts,

(Above) In southern France, sericulture was a well-established industry by the late eighteenth century. The French government supported and encouraged the production of silk in many ways. This Diderot illustration shows the reeling of silk cocoons. The standing woman turns the reel while the seated woman controls the number of filaments. (A Diderot Pictorial Encyclopedia of Trades and Industry.)

Traditional Japanese wheels that are used for twisting reeled silk.

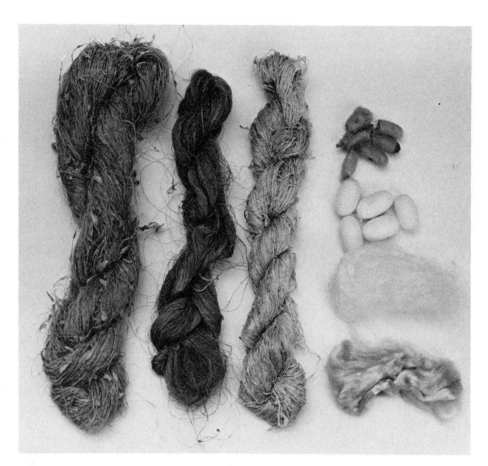

Silk fibers in various stages: cocoons; silk waste, or broken fibers; and skeins of spun silk.

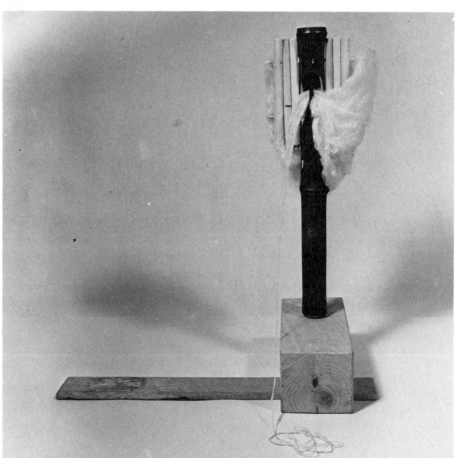

This Japanese tool, made of a bamboo pole mounted in a block of wood, serves as a holding device, or distaff, for silk fibers. The spinner draws the silk fibers out and rubs them between moistened thumb and finger, twisting first in one direction and then in the other.

first grasp two opposing corners and stretch the sheet out into a long, thin roving. Then spin the roving as you would wool. Sometimes the waste is a mass of short, light, airy fibers, which can be spun easily with no preparation. If the fibers are too long and tangled for easy spinning, they can be cut and teased.

Short silk fibers can be carded if a smooth yarn is desired. Since silk is very strong, the carding must be done lightly or the fibers will catch the teeth and prevent the cards from shifting. Silk also comes in a prepared, combed sliver, which can be easily spun into a smooth yarn. Sometimes the sliver is folded back and forth many times, and then compacted into a nice neat bundle, called a brick. After spinning, the twist can be set by spraying the silk skein with a mister, but this is usually not necessary.

Yarns from spun silk are different from those made from reeled silk. They are fuller, bulkier, and softer, with less luster (because there are more ends), less fineness, and less uniformity. Their softness makes these yarns a joy to deal with.

I have seen her spinning madly
    the worm's work into thread.
She sings a little out of key
    making ribbons for her head.

She will not buy silk from stores
    or at the market stand.
The only ribbons she adores
    are those she's made by hand.

Some like to work alone at night.
    Some choose to work in teams.
I see her now by lantern light
    spinning silk as soft as dreams.

Even a poet, when full grown,
    forgets his fondest memories.
Some never know the things they own
    were made by hands like these.

Homespun
(for Candace Crockett)
Ron Federighi

CHAPTER TEN

Advice From Experienced Spinners

How delightful to see,
In these evenings in spring,
The sheep going home to the fold.
The master doth sing,
As he views ev'rything,
And his dog goes before him where told,
And his dog goes before him where told.

The sixth month of the year,
In the month called June,
When the weather's too hot to be borne,
The master doth say,
As he goes on his way:
"Tomorrow my sheep shall be shorn,
Tomorrow my sheep shall be shorn."

Now as for those sheep,
They're delightful to see,
They're a blessing to a man on his farm.
For their flesh it is good,
It's the best of all food,
And the wool it will clothe us up warm . . .

Now, the sheep they're all shorn,
And the wool carried home,
Here's a health to our master and flock;
And if we should stay,
Till the last goes away,
I'm afraid 'twill be past twelve o'clock.

The Sheep-shearing
Eighteenth Century English Folk song

A. T. Spencer, breeder and developer of the Romeldale Sheep, was quoted in an interview in 1949 as saying, "We set out in 1915 to get a crossbred sheep which would produce a lamb able to handle our rough forage and not bloat up and die. . . . To start with, from the first crosses of Romney-Marsh and Rambouillet, I selected two families. It was slow progress, but at the end of ten years I had the head and body I was after in family number one, and the fleece in family number two. Then I interbred those two families to get the head, wool, and conformation of the Romeldale, and a new breed was born; the breed is fixed, there are no throwbacks."

As the various parts of this book fell together, there were bits and pieces that did not fit into the earlier chapters. This is where I have put those pieces—some too long for inclusion in earlier sections, others just little bits, not directly related to much of anything but sure to delight or interest the curious.

Some of the earlier paragraphs tell of the origins of sheep breeds. They are meant to encourage an appreciation for those who have increased the production and quality of wool and the strength and adaptability of the animal over the centuries. The following sections on the breeding and raising of sheep come from the personal recollections of Gloria Adamson and Anne Blinks, who continues her discussion of the breeding and caring for sheep.

RAISING SHEEP

Gloria Adamson continues to breed and raise sheep in that part of California where her grandfather, A.T. Spencer, perfected the Romeldale. Following are her recommendations:

I raise black sheep because raising them gives my spinning and weaving more meaning and gives me more control over the complete product. I also have the pleasure of providing quality fleece for other spinners as well as meat for my household. The whole process—from raising the sheep to spinning the yarn and then crocheting or weaving—gives me a great deal of satisfaction. It's a very special and complete experience. Some of my suggestions for the spinner who wants to start at the beginning follow.

First of all, find out which breeds do well in your geographical area. Then decide what kind of wool you want for your spinning.

Locate a breeder and buy good, healthy stock. If you only want one or two sheep and don't want to go into breeding, I would recommend wethers (castrated males), as they are calmer and easier to handle. Keep in mind that having three to four eyes may not necessitate purchasing a ram. Rams are sometimes difficult to handle and need separate pens or pasture when not being used for breeding. Sometimes you can borrow or rent a ram, or take your ewes to one for a couple of months. Remember, ewes should be bred every year as they may become sterile if they are not.

Raising sheep takes time—they don't take care of themselves. There will be *very* busy times, especially during lambing, shearing, and sickness, but, at all times, sheep have to be fed and watered every day. There are also all sorts of little things involving the health and care of the animal which must be done on a regular basis.

Before obtaining stock, check your local zoning laws to see whether sheep are allowed where you live, and what, if any, restrictions may be placed on their presence. Always think of the animals' comfort—never overcrowd them into a small pen. The soil will quickly become foul, the fleece dirty, and the area will be a bog in the rainy season. Remember that clean, quality fleece is your goal, and unhealthy living conditions will not produce it.

If you can provide pasture, have approximately six ewes per acre of good irrigated pasture in summer time, and two per acre in winter; for dry pasture, one ewe per acre year round is necessary. There should be enough room at water troughs, at feed racks, and in barns or sheds to prevent the sheep from crowding together—crowding is especially dangerous for pregnant

*Even though weaving had become a trade, most spinning in eighteenth-century pre-industrial France was still done in the home. The young girl on the left is spinning flax from a distaff to a hand spindle, while the woman on the right spins from distaff to wheel. The woman in Figure 3 is reeling yarn from a spindle into skeins, while the woman in Figure 4 winds skeined yarn from a swift into a ball. (*A Diderot Pictorial Encyclopedia of Trades and Industry.*)*

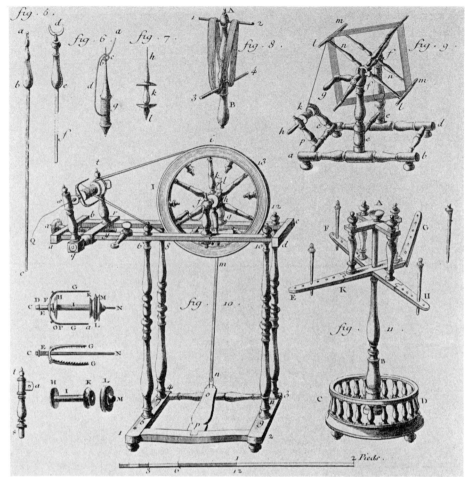

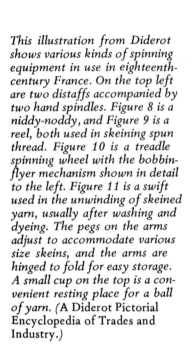

This illustration from Diderot shows various kinds of spinning equipment in use in eighteenth-century France. On the top left are two distaffs accompanied by two hand spindles. Figure 8 is a niddy-noddy, and Figure 9 is a reel, both used in skeining spun thread. Figure 10 is a treadle spinning wheel with the bobbin-flyer mechanism shown in detail to the left. Figure 11 is a swift used in the unwinding of skeined yarn, usually after washing and dyeing. The pegs on the arms adjust to accommodate various size skeins, and the arms are hinged to fold for easy storage. A small cup on the top is a convenient resting place for a ball of yarn. (A Diderot Pictorial Encyclopedia of Trades and Industry.)

ewes. It is better to understock than to overstock pastures. Sheep should be rotated from one field to another to allow the field to rest every two weeks or more. Sheep can also be kept in lots and fed hay and concentrates, but remember to allow plenty of room.

Fencing, shelter, feeding, and watering facilities should be built *before* getting the sheep. Estimate the maximum number of sheep you will have and build according-ly. I cannot stress the importance of good, dog-tight fencing—a dog attack can wipe out years of hard work in minutes. Posts of either wood or metal plus one stand of barbed wire at ground level, field or sheep fence for 36", and then two to three stands of barbed wire above are necessary. You can usual-ly obtain excellent plans for feeders, watering facilities, and

shelters from local county agricul-ture departments. Trace mineral salt and fresh water should be avail-able at all times. Good, well drained ground is a must, as wet, soggy soil invites foot problems, not to men-tion what it does to fleece.

Sheep need certain nutritional requirements that can be met in many different ways, depending on availability and amounts of feed. Check with the local agriculture man, the agriculture department at nearby colleges, veterinarians, 4-H people, and other sheep growers for the best types of feed in your area. Generally, I feed my sheep permanent pasture in summer and supplement with good quality alfafa, hay, and whole shelled corn in winter. I also give them molasses in the winter toward lambing time and increase carbohydrates. Ewes that are to be bred in the fall are flushed, or put on extra-good pasture 17 days or so prior to their being exposed to the ram for breeding—this increases the chances of twinning. Lambs are usually fed concentrates in a creep, an area with an entrance and exit large enough to allow them access but too small for the ewes to enter. Since the lambs are growing, this is essential.

Sheep raising is definitely not for the squeamish or the lazy. There are times of real need and emergency that necessitate quick, level-headed decisions. If the sight of blood and such upsets you, I would say don't bother. I have found this part, emergencies, the most educational of all my experiences—learning to treat wounds, give vaccinations, trim feet, dock tails, castrate, and on and on. The most rewarding of all experiences is helping a ewe give birth by giving assistance, the lack of which might have resulted in a dead lamb or ewe or both. Remember, sheep have been so domesticated by man that they are prone to a variety of troubles not found in their wild relatives. There is a regular yearly schedule of veterinary care consisting of lambing, worming, shearing, spraying or dipping, vaccination, and so on that becomes a regular routine of sheep raising.

The following publications contain especially helpful information for the sheep raiser. *Sheep and Wool Science* by Ensminger, an Interstate Printers Publication, is used as a college text. It is very thorough and covers the history and development of the sheep and goat industry, types and breeds of sheep, breeding, feeding, housing, equipment, health, diseases, and so on. It is written for the large sheep farm flock grower. *Approved Practices in Sheep Production*, by Juergenson, an Interstate publica-

tion, is a very good book which covers approximately the same material in abbreviated form. *Production Practices for California Sheep*, by Spurlock et al, manual #40, California Agricultural Extension service, is an excellent manual for beginners as it is well-illustrated and covers most areas beginners need to know about. It contains a pictorial lambing sequence that is very helpful.

One of the best books I have ever run across for the wool grower, especially the small flock owner, is a new publication by Paula Simmons, *Raising Sheep the Modern Way*, Garden Way Publishing, Charlotte, Vermont, 1976. The information is thorough, concise, and makes for excellent reading. The book also includes instructions for shearing with hand shears, tanning hides, treating manure for the garden, and rendering tallow for soup, soap, and candles, as well as various cooking recipes.

RAISING BLACK SHEEP

Anne Blinks is another Californian who raises her own sheep. Anne became fascinated with ancient textiles many years ago. After looking at museum collections and handmade items still in use in remote parts of the world, she decided that the only way to really understand those textiles was to reconstruct them. When she tried to find yarns to work with, she realized that proper yarns were just not available. This led her to spinning, but then she realized that proper fibers—black fibers that resemble those used by early people—were not available either. Anne quickly realized that the quality of both the fiber and the spinning were essential elements in the design, structure, and beauty of the textile pieces she was attempting to reconstruct. At that time there was

Spinning bees continue in many parts of the country and the world, offering many hours of pleasure. They provide not only for compatible and interesting gatherings, but also for the exchange of ideas and information. The forming threads bind people together in many ways.

little interest in black sheep, handspinning, or textiles, except on a commercial production basis. Today there is more interest and appreciation.

It is very important to remember the words in the little illustration from *Scottish Woollens*—"Keep the Quality Up." This involves thought, work, and time. What follows is an excerpt from Anne's experience with her black sheep. As well as being informative for the future sheep owner, it gives an indication of the commitment necessary to sheep raising as well as a feeling for the richness of experience and knowledge that can be obtained from deep involvement.

I have been raising black sheep for about 16 years. I say "about" because I made several false starts—perhaps I am still making them. I started out with Suffolks and soon decided they were not a wool sheep—that mistake shows how much I didn't know about sheep.

Next, I got a Rambouillet and used a good white Corriedale ram.

That gave me some blacks, surprisingly enough, in the first generation—to the horror of the breeder of the ram. However, the wool was too fine and much too short for my taste. Then I found a Hampshire ewe and a Columbia ewe, the latter of really good breeding, the former not so much, but of a lovely chocolate color. These two, bred to the Corriedale, gave me some really nice spinning wool. They are remarkably constant in the quality of the fleece and continue to shear well for several years. They also gave me seven out of eight black sheep year after year. This was all some 15 years ago. After a while I got board with these sheep and decided to try something different—but then I ran into troubles. The year before I switched to the Lincoln ram, I had a 200% lamb crop, raised to weaning. That went to my head, so I bought a fine, registered Lincoln from Don Kessi (a breeder in Oregon) and bred him to some black ewes (he was white but evidently heterozygous, as shown by the tiny black spots on his lips, tongue, and the skin of his ears). From the black ewes he gave us six whites, six blacks, and a pinto. But I lost two ewes just before lambing to "Pregnant Ewe Disease," and two more had to be rescued with molasses drenches. Two of the lambs were delivered by Caesarean and lived, but the mother never came out of the anesthesia. The two lambs that lived were black but both males.

Now I have seven half-Lincolns plus a few quarter-Lincolns, which are quite distinct from my essentially black Corriedales. I call the latter "Black Jacks" (from the hill on which we live, "Jacks Peak"). The wool from the Black Jacks is Corriedale in quality—fine for clothing and most weaving and knitting. The Corriedale wool is much longer (we shear twice a year), much blacker (not brownish), and much more lustrous and coarse. It is fine for wall hangings, tapestries, and rugs, but, by the third year the fleece gets very rough and coarse and begins to go gray. And the sheep are as big as Jerseys.

ONE WOMAN'S STORY

This letter, published in the August, 1974, issue of *The Web*, the quarterly journal of the New Zealand Spinning, Weaving, and Woolcrafts Society, shows the determination of one woman in learning to spin, and to work her spun yarn:

For eighteen years I lived in a remote area at the top on the Coromandel Peninsula. My son left home to work on a farm, and on one of his visits back to Port Charles, he spoke about women spinning their own wool. He was very keen for me to start spinning and, of course, he was thinking of all the warm work jerseys he could have in the cold

climate where he was working. Next thing I knew, I had the address of a gentleman in Wellington who made spinning wheels, and Chris [my son] sent me a little bulletin put out by the Agriculture Department on spinning and dyeing.

My wheel eventually arrived. It was complete with a flick carder, instructions how to use it, a Lazy Kate, and the bobbins on which were samples of wool beautifully spun by a 90-year-old man. So surely there was hope for me! Not being mechanically minded, I was a little frightened of the wheel, but my husband, who was interested, explained to me all the parts, and how and why they worked. For a fortnight I really tore at my hair trying to spin with the bulletin, plus wool, on my knee. Came the day when all of a sudden my feet, hands, wool and wheel just did exactly what they were supposed to do, and away I went.

I would spend a couple of hours each day spinning, and it wasn't long before the wool I was producing was not too bad. Someone told me about the Auckland Guild, so I wrote away and became an associate member. In those days the Guild sent out newsletters (these later became *The Web* and were handed to the N.Z.S.W.W.S. to produce—Ed.) On the days the mailman delivered them nothing was done until I had read them from beginning to end. How I looked forward to their arrival! I used to write to Jean Timlin with odd problems, and she always answered my letters promptly and made me feel that I really belonged to a group.

After a few months the dyeing bug got me. I started wandering through the bush and climbing

Spinning flax from a distaff on to a hand spindle. A loosely tied silk ribbon holds the long fibers in place on the distaff. A looped ribbon pinned to the spinner's shirt helps support the distaff, which is held under the arm.

the rocky coastline gathering dye materials. When visitors came to stay, they were taken on these excursions which they thoroughly enjoyed too.

With all this wool I was spinning and dyeing, what else could be done other than crochet and knitting. Of course, a loom. On a visit to Napier I acquired a thirty-two inch fixed-heddle table loom, also a copy of Simpson and Weir's book *The Weavers' Craft*. This time with book and loom on the floor, plus wool warps, my husband and I started to thread up using a little crochet hook to pull the warp threads through. Then the task of rolling on and crawling to bed in the small hours of the morning.

Once again the newsletters were invaluable and overcame a lot of my difficulties. Later on, other women in the area became interested, so I was able to help them in an elementary way. If there are women in remote areas who cannot get personal help, they can make the grade if they try hard enough, and if a husband or another member of the family is interested—two heads are better than one.

Living nearer civilization now

I really do enjoy belonging to a group and meeting people and exchanging ideas. Perhaps the odd copy of *The Web* could be forwarded to the postmistress or storekeeper in some of the remote places such as St. Barrier Island. Women could read them and perhaps start off a hobby which they thought beyond them.

June Barber,
Glenora Spinning Group,
South Auckland, New Zealand.

CONCLUSION

It would be as difficult to separate the mechanical art of spinning from its history as to separate the individual spinner from those many legions who since mankind's earliest days have worked to till the soil, sow and reap the crops, raise and shear the sheep, and sit, walk, and stand as they formed the individual strands into yarn. We must not forget that rather than being an appendage or addition to this long tradition, we are a natural and legitimate part of it—with our own songs, stories, and traditions, and our own way of seeking after higher quality, better materials, and the personal satisfaction that comes—that has always come—from completing a job well done. Happy spinning. . . .

KEEP THE QUALITY UP! KEEP THE QUALITY UP!!

Supplier's List

PERIODICALS
The periodicals listed below are likely to be of interest to the handspinner:

Black Sheep Newsletter
Route 2, Box 123-D Monroe
Oregon 97456
This newsletter contains helpful information. It will appeal to the handspinner and to the person interested in breeding and raising sheep.

Ciba Review
Ciba Ltd.
Basle, Switzerland
This scholarly journal has been published in English, German, French, and Italian since 1936. Not generally available outside library collections, it remains a consistently authoritative source of information on textiles.

Handweaver and Craftsman
220 Fifth Avenue
New York, New York 10001
Irregular publication dates and uneven quality since 1975. Prior to that most issues contained articles of interest to the handspinner.

Quarterly Journal Guilds
of Weavers Spinners and Dyers
6 Queen's Square
London, England WCIN 3AR
This British publication contains many articles on spinners and spinning.

The Shepherd
Sheffield, Massachusetts 02157
A sheep magazine, mainly of interest to sheep owners.

Shuttle Spindle and Dyepot
Handweavers Guild of American
998 Farmington Avenue
West Hartford, Connecticut 06107
This magazine regularly features articles on spinning and on spinning suppliers. Recent issues will have up to date want ads for all spinning needs.

Textile Museum Journal
The Textile Museum
2320 S Street, N.W.
Washington, D.C. 20008

The Web
P.O. Box 192
Cambridge, New Zealand
Contains many articles on spinners and spinning.

ANTIQUE SPINNING WHEELS
Information concerning the identification of antique wheels can be obtained from:

Mr. David A. Pennington
1993 West Liberty
Ann Arbor, Michigan 48103
Please send photographs of the wheel and rubbings of any identification marks. His book, American Spinning Wheels *(co-authored by M. Taylor), will also be helpful.*

COLLECTIONS
Although there are many museums and local historical societies that house special collections of handspinning tools, those listed below deserve special notice.

Bankfield Museum
Halifax, England

The British Museum
Department of Ethnography
6 Burlington Gardens
London, WI, England

John Horner Collection
Ulster Museum, Belfast, Ireland

Merrimack Valley Textile Museum
North Andover
Massachusetts

Pit Rivers Museum
Oxford, England

Science Museum
London, England

The Smithsonian Institution
Washington, D.C.

Upper Canada Village
St. Lawrence Parks Commission
Ontario, Canada

SPINNING SUPPLIERS
All of the following suppliers handle mail orders. Most of them have catalogs or brochures that are available at a nominal price and handle many different fibers, spindles, spinning wheels, and books. A notation is made below if only a particular item or kind of fiber is available. An asterisk indicates an especially complete and informative catalog.

Albion Hills Farm of Spinning
Route 3, Caledon East
Ontario, Canada

Spinning Wheel Kit
Ashford Handicrafts Ltd.
P.O. Box 12, Rakaia, New Zealand
This wheel is sold by many spinning suppliers, but if you are willing to wait about three months it can be ordered in kit form directly from New Zealand. The kit is inexpensive and very easy to assemble.

Bartlett Yarn, Inc.
Harmony, Maine 04942

Black Sheep
(Weaving and Craft Supply)
315 S.W. Third Street
Corvallis, Oregon 97330

C. Bailey
15 Dutton Street, Bankstown
NSW 2200, Australia
Full range of Australian fleece wools, as well as other fibers.

C. Fricke
Route 1, Box 143
Granite Falls, Washington 98252
Wool carding machine, hand wool carders.

C. Norman Hicks
4383 Piedmont Drive
San Diego, California 92107
Spinning wheels, including an electric spinner.

Casa De Las Tesedoras
1619 East Edinger
Santa Ana, California 92705

Clara Creager Co.
75 West College Ave.
Westerville, Ohio 43081

*Clemes & Clemes Spinning Wheels
665 San Pable Avenue
Pinole, California 94564

Creative Handweavers
P.O. Box 26480
Los Angeles, California 90026
This general supplier also carries the Pakistani spinner and the Gandhi charka.

Colonial Textiles
82 Plants Dam Road
East Lyme, Connecticut 06333

*Colorado Fleece Company
grease wool—516 West Ute Avenue
Grand Junction, Colorado 81501
other fibers—Rita Forte, Route 1
Box 174, Palisade, Colorado 81526

Columbine Machine Shop
1835 South Acoma Street
Denver, Colorado 80223
All-metal spinning wheel.

Custom Handweavers—
Allied Arts Guild
Arbor at Creek Road
Menlo Park, California 94025

The Darby Ram
5056 Lee Highway
Arlington, Virginia

Davidson's Old Mill Yarn
109 Elizabeth Street, Box 8
Eaton Rapids, Michigan 48827

Dick Blick
Dept. 11, Box 1267
Galesburg, Illinois 61401

E.B. Frey & Son, Inc.
Wilton, New Hampshire 03086
Handcarders.

Earth Guild, Inc.
149 Putnam Avenue
Cambridge, Massachusetts 02139

Frederick J. Fawcett, Inc.
129 South Street
Boston, Massachusetts 02111
Flax line for spinning.

Gallery One
Mercado Plaza, 800 Rio Grande, N.W.
Albuquerque, New Mexico 87106

Gordon's Naturals
P.O. Box 506
Roseburg, Oregon 97470

*Greentree Ranch Wools
& Countryside Handweavers
163 North Carter Lake Road
Loveland, Colorado 80537

Guild of Shaker Crafts
401 West Savidge Street
Spring Lake, Michigan 49456

*Handcraft Wools
Box 378, Streetsville
Ontario, Canada

The Handweaver
1643 San Pable Avenue
Berkeley, California 94702

The Handweaver
460 First Street East, Box 1271
Sonoma, California 95476

Handweavers of Los Altos
305 State Street
Los Altos, California 94022

Harrisville Designs
Harrisville, New Hampshire 03450

*Hedgehog Equipment
Wheatcroft, Itchingfield
Horsham, Sussex, England
Full range of English fleece wools, as well as other fibers. Drum carder, card clothing, and various other supplies.

The Hidden Village
215 Yale Avenue
Claremont, California 91711

Historick Arkaeologisk Forsøgscenter
Lejre, 4000 Roskilde, Denmark
Wool combs.

Intertwine
217 Trolley Square
Salt Lake City, Utah 84102

J. L. Hammet Co.
48 Canal Street
Boston, Massachusetts 02114

*Jones Sheep Farm
R.R. 2, Peabody, Kansas 66866

Laurence Whalen
6335 Striker Road
Maineville, Ohio 45039
Romney wool.

Lily Mills Company
Department HWEA, Box 88
Shelby, North Carolina 28150
Cotton fibers.

The Linders
1347 San Miguel
Phoenix, Arizona
Cotton fibers, seeds, and roving.

Magnolia Weaving
2635 29th Avenue
West Seattle, Washington 98199

*The Mannings
East Berlin, Pennsylvania 17316

The Pendleton Shop
Box 233, 407 Jordon Road
Sedona, Arizona 86336

Robin and Russ Handweavers
533 North Adams Road
McMinnville, Oregon 97128

Richardson Studio
1932 Emerson Street
Palo Alto, California 94301

The River Farm
Route 1, Box 169 A
Timberville, Virginia 22853
Fleece.

The Rug Hut
6 University Avenue
Los Gatos, California 95020

Schneider and Krieger
Bay Street Village
Bellingham, Washington 98225

School Products Co., Inc.
1201 Broadway
New York, New York 10001

Serendipity Shop
1547 Ellinwood
Des Plaines, Illinois 60016

*Shaw Island Fleece Co.
3413 Fremont Avenue North
Seattle, Washington 98103

Marguerite Shimmin
2470 Queensberry Road
Pasadena, California 91104
Silkworm eggs.

Silver Shuttle
1301 35th Street, N.W.
Washington, D.C. 20007

*Some Place
2990 Adeline
Berkeley, California 94703

Spider Web
803 South Fort Harrison
Clearwater, Florida 33516

Spincraft
Box 332
Richardson, Texas 75080

The Spinning Wheel
130 Church Street
San Francisco, California 94114

The Spinster
34 Hamilton Avenue
Sloatsburg, New York 10974

*Straw Into Gold
P.O. Box 2904
550a College Avenue
Oakland, California 94618

The Thread Mill
111 East University Drive
Tempe, Arizona 85281

Traditional Handcrafts
571 Randolph Street
Northville, Michigan 48167

Walter Kircher
335 Marburg/Lahn
Postfach 1408, West Germany

Watson
P.O. Box 12231
Wellington, New Zealand
Full range of New Zealand fleece.

Yarn Barn
730 Massachusetts, Box 344
Lawrence, Kansas 66044

Yarn Box
P.O. Box 1428
Jonesboro, Arkansas 72401

Yarn Depot
545 Sutter Street
San Francisco, California 94102

The Yarnery
1648 Grand Avenue
St. Paul, Minnesota 55105

Weaver's Place
Dickey Mill
4900 Wetheredsville Road
Baltimore, Maryland 21204

The Weaver's Shop
39 Courtland, Box 457
Rockford, Michigan 49341

The Weaver's Store
271 Amburn Street
Newton, Massachusetts 02166

Wool 'N' Shop
(North Central Wool Marketing Corp.)
101 27th Avenue S.E.
Minneapolis, Minnesota 55414

Sally White
Route 3, Scio, Oregon 97374
Fleece.

Bibliography

Baines, P., and Roberts, M. "Survey of Handspinning for Weaving." *Quarterly Journal The Guilds of Weavers Spinners and Dyers,* Autumn, 1973.

Blackburn, Edna. "Breeds of Sheep." *Shuttle, Spindle, and Dyepot,* Spring, 1972.

Boyd, Ruth. "Characteristics of Wool." *Handweaver and Craftsman,* October, 1975.

British Sheep Breeds, Their Wool and Its Uses. Middlesex, England: The British Wool Marketing Board.

Burnham and Burnham. *'Keep Me Warm one Night.'* Toronto: University of Toronto Press, 1973.

Chamberlain, Marcia, and Crockett, Candace. *Beyond Weaving.* New York: Watson-Guptill Publications, 1974.

Channing, Marion. *The Textile Tools of Colonial Homes.* Marion Channing, 1969.

Chapin, Doloria M. *Single Thread Yarns.* Fabius, New York: Doloria Chapin, 1974.

Chapin, Doloria. *Spinning Around the World, International Handspinning Directory and Handbook.* Fabius, New York: Doloria Chapin, 1975.

Chesley, Zina Mae. "Hand-Carding by Machine." *Shuttle, Spindle and Dyepot,* June, 1970.

Crawford, M.D.C. *The Heritage of Cotton.* New York: Fairchild Publishing Co., 1948.

Crowfoot, Grace M. *Methods of Hand Spinning in Egypt and the Sudan.* Halifax, England: Bankfield Museum, 1931.

Davenport, Elsie. *Your Handspinning.* Pacific Grove, California: Craft and Hobby Book Service, 1968.

Diderot, Denis. *A Diderot Pictorial Encyclopedia of Trades and Industry.* Edited with Introduction and Notes by Charles C. Gillespie. Volume Two. New York: Dover Publications Inc., 1959.

Eaton, Peaches. "A Grand Old Spinner and Weaver." *The Web,* August, 1974.

Edgerton, Kate. "Buying an Old Spinning Wheel." *Shuttle, Spindle, and Dyepot,* December, 1969.

Edgerton, Kate. "Reconditioning Wheels." *Shuttle, Spindle and Dyepot,* June, 1970.

Exner, Beatrice B. "Acadian Brown Cotton." *Handweaver and Craftsman,* Fall, 1960.

Fannin, Allen. *Handspinning.* New York: Van Nostrand Reinhold, 1970.

——————. "Hand Spinning for the Seventies." *Craft Horizons,* February, 1971.

——————. "Proper Preparation of Fibers for Spinning." *Handweaver and Craftsman,* Summer, 1969.

——————. "Spinning Flax." *Handweavers and Craftsman,* Spring, 1967.

Gilbert, K.R. *Textile Machinery.* London: Her Majesty's Stationery Office, 1971.

Grassett, K. *Complete Guide to Hand Spinning.* Pacific Grove, California: Craft and Hobby Book Service, 1971.

Gray, Andrew. *Spinning Machinery.* Edinburgh: Archibald Constable and Comp., 1819.

Gutman, A. L. "Cloth Making in Flanders." *Ciba Review,* October, 1938.

Held, Shirley E. *Weaving.* New York: Holt, Rinehart and Winston, 1973.

Hicks, Norman C. "Spindle." *Shuttle, Spindle, and Dyepot,* Summer, 1975.

Hochberg, Bette. *Handspinner's Handbook.* Santa Cruz, California: Hochberg, 1976.

Hollen, N., and Sadler, J. *Textiles.* New York: Macmillan, 1968, Third Edition.

Hyatt, Rebecca. *Mary Lou's Kiverlid.* Morristown, Tennessee: Morrison Printing Co., 1963.

Johnson, George H. *Textile Fabrics.* New York: Harper and Brothers, 1927.

Juergenson, Elwood. *Approved Practices in Sheep Production.* Danvill, Illinois: The Interstate, 1973.

Kent, Kate Peck. *The Cultivation and Weaving of Cotton in the Prehistoric Southwestern United States.* Philadelphia: The American Philosopical Society, 1957.

King, Mary E. *Ancient Peruvian Textiles.* New York: The Museum of Primitive Art, 1965.

Kluger, M. *The Joy of Spinning.* New York: Simon and Schuster, 1971.

Leggett, William. *The Story of Linen.* New York: Chemical Publishing Co., 1945.

Leix, Alfred. "Weaving and Dyeing in Ancient Egypt and Babylon." *Ciba Review,* August, 1938.

Marten, Eileen. "Drum Carding." *The Web,* March, 1975.

Mathieson, Ian. "Choosing a Spinning Wheel." *The Web,* March, 1974.

_____ . "The Spinning Wheel." *The Web,* June, 1974.

_____ . "The Spinning Wheel." *The Web,* August, 1974.

Mathews, J.M. *The Textile Fibres.* New York: John Wiley and Sons, 1916.

Neumann, Erich. *The Great Mother.* New York: Pantheon Books, 1955.

Parslow, Virginia. "Flax From Seed to Yarn." *Handweaver and Craftsman,* Spring, 1952.

Pendleton, Mary. *Navajo and Hopi Weaving Techniques.* New York: Macmillan, 1974.

Pennington, D. and Taylor, M. *American Spinning Wheels.* Sabbathday Lake, Maine: Shaker Press, 1975.

Pentler, Fumiko. "Raising Silkworms." *Handweaver and Craftsman,* Winter, 1969.

_____ . *Silk.* Cupertino, California: Pentler, 1971.

Ponting, K.G. "Early Handspinning Wheels." *Quarterly Journal The Guilds of Weavers Spinners and Dyers,* June, 1966.

Roth, H. Ling. *Hand Card Making.* Halifax, England: Bankfield Museum.

_____ . *Hand Woolcombing.* Halifax, England: Bankfield Museum.

Schwartz, A. "The Reel." *Ciba Review,* August, 1947.

Scottish Woollens. Published by the National Association of Scottish Woolen Manufacturers: 1956.

Shaefer, G. "Flax and Hemp." *Ciba Review,* April, 1945.

Silk: The World of Silk. New York: American Fabrics.

Simmons, Paula. "Carding by Machine." *Handweaver and Craftsman,* Summer, 1969.

_____ . "How to Raise Sheep." *Handweaver and Craftsman,* Spring, 1971.

_____ . "How to Raise Sheep: Advice for Ambitious Spinners, Part II. " *Handweaver and Craftsman,* Summer, 1971.

_____ . *Raising Sheep the Modern Way.* Charlotte, Vermont: Garden Way Publishing, 1976.

Sitaramayya, Dr. Paltabhi. *I Too Have Spun.* Bombay: Hind Kitabs Limited, 1946.

South, Stanley. "The Lowly Flax Hackle." *Antiques,* August, 1968.

Spencer, Audrey, *Spinning and Weaving at Upper Canada Village.* Toronto: Ryerson Press, 1964.

"Spinning Survey." *The Web,* December, 1970.

"The Spinning Wheel." *Ciba Review,* No. 28.

Spurlock, G.M. "Inheritance of Coat Color in Sheep." *Black Sheep Newsletter,* Issue 4, Summer, 1975.

Teal, Peter. "Wool Combing." *Quarterly Journal The Guilds of Weavers, Spinners and Dyers,* Autumn, 1974.

Teller, Walter Magnes. *Starting Right With Sheep.* Charlotte, Vermont: Garden Way Publishing, 1975.

"Textiles in Biblical Times." *Ciba Review,* No. 2, 1968.

Thompson, G. B. *Spinning Wheels (The John Horner Collection).* Belfast: Ulster Museum, 1966.

Varron, A. "The European Carpet." *Ciba Review,* July, 1939.

Weir, Shelagh. *Spinning and Weaving in Palestine.* London: The British Museum, 1970.

Wehrlin, Max. "Raw Silk for the Handweaver." *Handweaver and Craftsman,* Spring, 1955.

Wescher, H. "Great Masters of Dyeing in 18th Century France." *Ciba Review,* February, 1939.

Wittlin, A. "The Development of the Textile Crafts in Spain." *Ciba Review,* April, 1939.

Wool Knowledge: The Journal of Wool Education. Department of Education of the International Wool Secretariat, London 1962.

Index

Edited by Ellen Zeifer
Designed by Bob Fillie
Composed in 12 point Aldine Roman by Copy Prep Company
Printed and bound by Interstate Book Manufacturers
Color printed by Toppan Printing Co. (America) Ltd.

818243
M

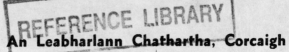

REFERENCE LIBRARY

An Leabharlann Chathartha, Corcaigh

CORK CITY LIBRARY

CENTRAL LIBRARY
GRAND PARADE

REFERENCE DEPARTMENT

CLASS R 738·2099 / SOT A/NO N. 140124

THIS BOOK is provided for use in the Reference Room
only, and must not be taken away. It is earnestly
requested that readers use the books with care, and
do not soil them, or cut, tear or turn down leaves, or
write or make any marks on them or otherwise damage
them. The habit of wetting finger or thumb to turn
leaves should especially be avoided. The use of the
Reference Room is subject to the Rules and Bye-Laws;
and any injury to books, or any improper conduct,
will be dealt with as therein provided.

SBN